# SHADOW MIGRATION

*American Lives*
Series editor: Tobias Wolff

# Shadow Migration

## MAPPING A LIFE

Suzanne Ohlmann

University of Nebraska Press
LINCOLN

An earlier version of chapter 8, "Doppelgänger," first
appeared as "An Addict, a Nurse, and a Christmas
Resurrection." © 2019 Suzanne Ohlmann. First
published in Longreads, http://www.longreads.com.

Bill Kloefkorn's "Nebraska: This Place, These
People" originally appeared in Nebraska: This Place,
These People (Norfolk NE: Nebraska Life Publishing,
2010) and appears courtesy of Eloise Kloefkorn.

Library of Congress Cataloging-in-Publication Data
Names: Ohlmann, Suzanne, author.
Title: Shadow migration: mapping
a life / Suzanne Ohlmann.
Description: Lincoln: University of Nebraska
Press, [2022] | Series: American lives
Identifiers: LCCN 2021043714
ISBN 9781496226860 (paperback)
ISBN 9781496231161 (epub)
ISBN 9781496231178 (pdf)
Subjects: LCSH: Ohlmann, Suzanne. | Adoptees—United
States—Biography. | Musicians—United States—
Biography. | Nurses—United States—Biography. | BISAC:
BIOGRAPHY & AUTOBIOGRAPHY / Personal Memoirs
Classification: LCC CT275.O4453 A3 2022 |
DDC 306.874092 [B]—dc23/eng/20211014
LC record available at https://lccn.loc.gov/2021043714

Set in Quadraat by Mikala R. Kolander.
Designed by N. Putens.

To Grandma A, who so loved words

. . . the wind sprang up afresh, with a kind of bitter song, as if it said: "This is reality, whether you like it or not. All those frivolities of summer, the light and shadow, the living mask of green that trembled over everything, they were lies, and this is what was underneath. This is the truth."

—WILLA CATHER, My Ántonia

# Contents

# Author's Note

This book was written from my point of view and is a work of creative nonfiction. Some names have been changed to protect the identities of the people involved. The facts remain facts—where I was born, who made me, where I landed. But my experience inside of those facts is my own, and I hope you'll trust me as your guide. Thank you.

# SHADOW MIGRATION

# 1

## Gin

Alone in his bed, a fifty-one-year-old man dies in a Phoenix suburb trailer park. As his soul rises from his body, it transforms into a luminous orb and shoots like a star across the western sky. It's late December and he's my father, though unknown to me. His death will go unnoticed for days.

Nearly twenty-five hundred miles to the north and east, I sit in a black velvet dress sipping Malbec at a Lincoln Center bar off Broadway and Sixty-Fifth Street. The afterglow of the opera shines like a halo around me. I've got a major crush on the bass-baritone who commanded the evening's performance, and I learn from the bartender that said hunk is in a booth at the back of the restaurant. I close my tab and add a tall of Himself's favorite drink to the bill before settling up.

Buzzed with wine and music and youth, I miss the ball of light that sails past my face and clinks into the glass as the bartender mixes Himself's gin and tonic. As I put on my coat, I note a towering figure approaching from the back, drink in hand, lime in drink, and I realize he's looking not past me but at me, eyes locked.

First he thanks me for the drink. Then he offers me a taste. I sip, then he sips. We gaze at each other amidst the epic sipping, and the fate of our weekend is sealed. In an hour he'll sweep me into a kiss in the stinging cold outside of the next bar. At his apartment, he'll play Ella Fitzgerald and we'll dance, my toes on his feet with each step.

He feels like the magic of life condensed into one perfect being, his kisses a combination of humility and passion, not the grody tongue excavations I've survived in the past. For twelve hours we wander together through the rose-hued fantasy of instant romance.

My father never knew he had me. But that weekend, on his way to an eternal rest, he sought means beyond comprehension and, in the breath and embrace of Himself, held me the way I'd been seeking my whole life—a way that made me ache with loss. I wasn't raised to believe in reincarnation, but that gin and tonic I shared with Himself forced me to consider the possibility, in life, in my life, within me, within all of us, of the transmigration of souls.

# 2

# Thunder Road

We don't talk about loss in my family, but I've always been told that my great-grandpa Ohlmann died of a broken heart. After he lost his central Nebraska farm to the Great Depression and moved to town, he did little else but sit and smoke on a chair out back, while Great-Grandma took in renters and washed clothes. It was the early 1940s when Katherine Ohlmann delivered laundry in Kearney, Nebraska, walking with purpose from house to house with stacks of folded shirts and linens, a large hat with a protuberant feather perched atop her head. She must have been a fixture in the daily life of her neighborhood, the hard-working, Lutheran farm wife with the lost farm and the husband, Dietrich, hidden behind the house.

I have another family, in addition to the Ohlmanns, who also hails from central Nebraska. Thirty years after Great-Grandma Katherine walked Kearney's streets in her feathered hat, my biological father did the same, and just as noticeably. Skinny and tall, with a mullet of dusty brown hair, he skipped the hat and went straight for 1970s hippy fashion: American flag pants. His name was Mike, and he drove a pea-green, two-door, 1974 Chevy Vega wagon. When he picked up a girl for a date—and he had plenty of dates—crushed beer cans would spill out of the passenger side of the car as soon as she opened the door.

My dad, Glenn Ohlmann, took me to Kearney in 1987 for my great-aunt Hulda's funeral. I was in sixth grade. At the age of twelve, I knew nothing about my flag-panted biological father and certainly nothing about beer. My parents, Glenn and Pat, also Lutherans, have the same liquor in their cupboard that they've had since Lyndon Johnson was president. Grandpa Ohlmann, Dad's dad and son of Katherine and Dietrich, attended Hulda's funeral and offered my dad his token moment of family funeral embarrassment. Grandpa O liked to take pictures of dead people in caskets, and he did so with the same gusto as his mother had when she delivered laundry. He used a fancy camera with a giant, detachable flash, which he engaged while taking the photos. This horrified Dad, a man who always tried to avoid attracting attention.

It would seem that my biological father didn't mind attention in the least, what with the showy pants and the clatter of cans that accompanied his outings. He represented a Kearney, a Nebraska, that I'd never imagined growing up ninety miles east in the rituals of my Ohlmann family, which included Lutheran church, Lutheran school, tithing, Bible verses, Jell-O salad, and Bach cantatas. In the summer of 1975, the summer I was made, the summer Bruce Springsteen released Thunder Road, Mike was nineteen and throwing wild parties, dating two women (at least), and shooting heroin at the kitchen table, while my parents were planting a garden, teaching vacation bible school, and reading Richard Scarry books to my soon-to-be big brother, aged four at the time. Mike and Leah, my biological mother, were in summer love, or so Leah thought, and over the Fourth of July weekend, in an act of true patriotism, they climbed into the back of his Vega and conjured me into earthly existence.

But Mike turned his attention to another woman, Karen, and Leah went the way of the clattering cans. Soon after, Mom and Dad decided they wanted to adopt a child, and they began meeting with Lutheran Family Services in Lincoln. Then Leah missed her period and Mike's Vega burst into flames in front of Karen's house, like Springsteen's "skeleton frames of burned out Chevrolets." With the evidence of my origins burned to a crisp and Leah away in Grand Island to hide her pregnancy (she didn't tell him), it's a wonder I ever discovered any remnant of Mike. He didn't die in the Vega fire, but the slow deterioration of his life began that summer of 1975.

Mike's shadow would follow me for thirty years, until I finally returned to his memory and the Kearney he knew, a place far outside the brick walls of the Zion Lutheran Church there on Highway 30, where I stood at age twelve and cringed with my Dad while Grandpa O snapped a picture of dead Hulda in the casket. My eyes swam with blue spots from the camera's flash. Or could those lights have been from Mike's car driving past outside? What if our paths had crossed that day, or on other trips to Kearney over the years of my childhood, neither of us aware of the other's existence? Might Mike have seen me through the church doors for that split second? Could he have known that the girl in the corduroy jumper and pink knee socks just next to the casket was his lost daughter? I'll never know. I couldn't see.

By all accounts, Mike had a sunny disposition, and so do I, both of us with big smiles showing ample teeth. We're catalysts for connection who treat strangers like long-lost friends. We remember people's birthdays and are the first to call a loved one in need. But how to explain the beer and the heroin? Who struts down Main Street in the Stars and Stripes, then ties on a tourniquet and shoots heroin into his veins with a shared needle? Was Mike merely a product of the cavalier seventies, or did shadows haunt him as they later did me?

Mike died at age fifty-one at the Sunshine Valley Mobile Home Park in Chandler, Arizona, alone and unaware of what his loins had wrought that fateful summer of '75. He was found in bed days later after a neighbor noticed packages piling up outside his door. When I visited the trailer park, more than ten years after his death, a burst of white petunias sprang from underneath his former front bedroom. I wanted to crawl past the flowers and bury myself there, under the house. I'd finally found communion in the sanctity of the remnants of his life: desert dust, corrugated metal, a stranger's home, flowers.

In his final months, Mike spent each day hungover, then set out at night with cash to pay the girls at the local bar to dance with him. He paid extra to those who were single mothers. When I searched for that bar and found myself in a grill supply store across from Sunshine Valley, the owner, an older man, mopped the floor while I told him the Cliff's Notes version of my story.

"No bars around here, but we do share a driveway with Sonny's."

"Sonny's?" I asked.

"Was a cowboy bar in the '80s."

"And now?"

He stopped mopping.

"Strip club."

*Duh*, I thought. Strip clubs—not bars—staff dancers.

I didn't come to this conclusion on my own, because I was raised by Lutherans in rural Nebraska. Despite my own colorful past—see binge drinking (don't drunk-text your boss, and when you do, don't call him "turd face," and when you type "turd," don't misspell it t-e-r-d), torrid affairs with married men, and a brush with suicide—I continued to perceive the world through the naiveté of my Lutheran subculture. Parents who drink liquor on an every-other-decade basis, who spend years of their life singing in four-part harmony, and whose single classroom rule through forty-plus years of teaching is "Be appropriate" raise children who are slow to realize that the reason they suffer increasingly grave bouts of depression might be because they were born—by accident—to two flailing, potentially depressive, potentially addictive young people in the midst of a decade of free love, acid trips, and heroin that traveled from the jungles of Vietnam to the windy plains of Nebraska.

In spite of all the staid behavior instilled by the Ohlmanns, however, I walked my days with a secret: my heart was broken, too, just like my great-grandpa Ohlmann's. If I didn't take the risk to dig into the past, I'd be on the road to a life shortened by sadness, much like Mike. Somehow I had to find a way to reconcile the hymns of my childhood with the Old Milwaukee that killed my father.

# 3

## *Magnum* PI

Though the beginning of my life may read to an adult like a smoothly planned itinerary—nine months inside of my mother, three days in the hospital, six days in the hands of Lutheran Family Services, and finally my delivery into the arms of the Ohlmanns—the trajectory and impact must have been jarring to a thin-skinned neonate, like being catapulted from a realm of chaos and heartbreak into an alternate universe of calm and predictability.

I didn't actually land, of course, but was placed there in a ceremony at the Lincoln offices of LFS, with a pastor, the social worker who placed me (Gary), and my family all present. In photographs documenting the adoption, my parents are smiling through their panic and 1970s bowl cuts, my brother is looking shy with his blond bangs and dark-rimmed glasses askew, and me, with my shock of dark brown hair and eyes closed, I'm fast asleep. I must have been exhausted.

I imagine it felt to that tiny baby like an arrival by way of Der Viener Schlinger, the air-powered cannon at University of Nebraska football games that fires Fairbury brand hot dogs from the field to hungry fans seated as high as the upper deck. I picture my social worker, Gary, picking me up from the hospital in Grand Island. He tightens my swaddle, gives me a couple of loving pats, and packs me into Der Viener Schlinger's launching chamber. Safely loaded, Gary hikes the hot dog–shaped bazooka onto his shoulder, aims east toward Seward, and ka-WAMP!, launches me toward my new home, where Mom and Dad stand in the yard, arms outstretched, waiting for me to sail over the roof of St. Andrew's Church next door.

"I'm a brother! I'm a brother!" My brother points to me sailing through the sky as he jumps up and down.

Mom catches me (she is the athlete in the family, her nose just a touch crooked from a softball injury), hands me to Dad, and my new family performs a careful inspection.

"Well, Glenn," Mom says, "she looks appropriate, and it's nearly five o'clock. I'd better get in to start supper." She takes me from Dad and walks toward the house. Their new addition has arrived safely, and they fall back into the schedule they've kept for the twelve years of their marriage, each of them expecting that I'll do the same.

And so the tidy lawns and clean-swept walks of Seward became home. My dad is no exception to the many in town who rush out to pick up twigs from the yard after a storm and shovel snow as the flakes fall, "just in case somebody needs to get past." A Romanesque, domed courthouse sits on the town square, surrounded by brick streets and local shops. Besides Concordia University and its music, art, and sports programs, we had a community swimming pool shaped like a big, blue bowl, a public park with gleaming ball fields, and a Dairy Queen. Mixing Blizzards at the DQ gave a sense of purpose to my teenage self, and I thrilled to turn them upside down for mildly amused customers (these are Nebraskans, mind you—nobody gets too excited about anything).

In 1974 a local artist and Concordia professor named Reinhold Marxhausen and his students created a mural on the side of one of downtown Seward's corner buildings. They painted a striking image of Nebraska's agricultural identity, with swaths of earth layered in deep, jewel tones across the length of the building and part of a poem by Nebraska poet William Kloefkorn printed atop the rich colors:

Nebraska,
Water and soil and wind,

Color and light and heat:
Something forever plump and firm,
Above the ground,
The itch forever.
Of something small but ripening,
Underneath.

I lived just seven blocks north of Marxhausen's mural when I was growing up, in a brick house with a screened-in porch on the corner of Fifth and Hillcrest. I could have ridden my bike to work downtown, but a car was a much cooler mode of transportation for a Seward teenager, so I drove the 1984 Mazda pick-up I shared with my dad. It was no hotrod, but I felt quietly proud of its four-on-the-floor transmission and lack of power steering.

Nebraskans are quietly proud about many things. We don't want to draw attention to ourselves or give the impression we think we're better than anyone else. You'll know us best through our work, an aspect of Plains life that is never really finished. My dad is notorious for sitting down to supper after a day full of lawn mowing, gutter repair, removal of an entire hackberry tree, and the cataloging of three crates of books and saying, "Good grief," as he drops his head into his heads, "I haven't gotten a thing done today."

But we love to work. Just give us a task and we'll keep our heads down and do it. That's why every small cone I served during my three years at the Dairy Queen weighed exactly five ounces, the weight I was trained to serve using an old-fashioned kitchen scale under the watchful eye of my manager, Marilyn. Marilyn didn't suffer fools and could spot an oversized cone from across the restaurant. So even if you were a good friend and we'd sat by each other in Spanish class all sophomore year, I wouldn't have made your cone any bigger. That's just how things are done in Nebraska. We don't want anyone to think they're too special.

My family gave me ample opportunities to feel special, but not *too* special, throughout my childhood. My grandma made me tart apple pie on my birthday, with enough zing to make your cheeks pucker. My grandpa brought me Doublemint gum in the breast pocket of his suit, teasing me as I gazed up with hopeful eyes when he fumbled around in the pockets, a look of feigned panic on his face as if he'd forgotten my favorite thing. He never forgot. My parents read to me before sleep, mixed Nestle Quik into the milk in my Miss Piggy glass at suppertime, and drove my big brother and me across America in our Dodge station wagon on summer vacations, stopping for ice cream in every town where we stayed. My childhood in Seward glimmered with all the signs of a well-organized, well-intentioned life with two educated, employed parents who stayed together, a big brother who watched out for me, fun-loving aunts and uncles, and a set of cousins I idolized, partly because they were older than I was and partly because they lived in exotic cities like Minneapolis and Boulder.

At St. John, my grade school, I memorized Bible verses, carried candles in the Christmas Eve service, and babysat my teacher's kids on weeknights so they could go to church meetings and sing in the choir.

I rode bikes with friends, saw the seven o'clock movie on Fridays at the Rivoli, and learned to make hot pads and elastic-waist skirts in sewing classes at the Fabric Fair store.

I earned straight As.

I wrote thank-you notes.

I did everything right.

But if you'd stayed at the Dairy Queen past closing time during the summer after I turned sixteen, you'd have seen me walking to my pick-up, visor off, Hot Eats/Cool Treats T-shirt untucked. By the time I climbed in and reached to strap on my seat belt, I'd be crying so hard I'd have to rest my head on the steering wheel. After a few minutes, I'd reach for the scratchy paper napkins in the glove box to wipe the Wet n Wild mascara from my cheeks.

I cried about the little boy I babysat, toddling around with a belly full of cancer, soon to lose a kidney, start chemotherapy, and then what?

I cried about my aunt and uncle on the cusp of divorce. Both were teachers and churchgoers, and they took their role as my godparents seriously, assuring me on every visit that they were there for me, that I would be okay in life, that I would make it. But if they didn't make it, how could I?

I cried about the newly graduated senior from school who'd come through the DQ drive-through that day so he could yell "Bitch!" over his car CB radio as he passed by me in the open window. He'd done the same thing the week before while driving past our house on Hillcrest. My dad, consumed with mowing the side yard in crisp, diagonal rows, had missed the whole thing. As I weeded my mom's flowerbeds, I crouched in horror, wondering if I could just dig a shallow grave and slip in. That boy's cruelty should have angered me, but I felt scared and isolated instead.

At the end of the previous school year, my sophomore year, without meaning to, I'd blown the whistle on a friend of mine, the joker from the senior class of our four hundred–student high school. Around noon on the last Monday of the year, I'd finished lunch and walked into the band room to get my bass guitar ready for jazz band.

"Hey, Suzy! Look!" laughed the joker. He sat with a group of guys in the middle of the room and pointed at his crotch. His other hand held the leg of his shorts open, the band room's fluorescent lights shining down on the wrinkly skin of his privates.

I rolled my eyes, kept walking, and tried to pretend nothing had happened.

More laughter.

I'd never seen a scrotum before. I probably couldn't have told you the proper name for that part of the male genitalia if you'd asked. And worse, I couldn't believe the joker had chosen to introduce me to his scrotum in jazz band that day. I was the girl from his grade school and church; the girl whose family had joined his to attend piano recitals, outdoor theater productions, and Lincoln Symphony Orchestra concerts; the girl who'd taken piano lessons from his mother every week since second grade; the girl who'd played violin with him every Saturday morning in youth orchestra. Why me? Why anyone? Who wants to see genitals in the band room after lunch? Or ever?

He flashed two more girls before the band teacher showed up.

After school we three girls stood around our lockers venting about the ordeal. One of the guidance counselors passed by and overheard enough to know something was wrong. But we didn't know that if a guidance counselor overhears students talking about something illegal, she's required by law to report it. We didn't know that flashing your genitals in jazz band was illegal.

I didn't know that I would come home that evening from a piano lesson at the joker's house and find a police officer sitting with my parents at our dining room table. The other girls didn't take piano from the joker's mom. I don't know when the police went to their houses.

I didn't know that I didn't have to file a report or that by writing out the sequence of events with the police officer's help, that's precisely what I was doing. (Despite eighth grade health class, I wasn't sure how to spell genitals or what exactly a scrotum was, and when she asked if I'd seen the shaft, I nearly sank under the table. You don't want to learn those words from a cop. I think this was why she hugged me before she left.)

I didn't know that because of my police report, the joker would be prosecuted, that he'd be suspended from his last week of school, miss graduation, and receive what seemed to me a new, higher social status for all the punishment he suffered. Meanwhile, I lost my place in the social order, as demonstrated by being called a bitch over loud speakers by one of the joker's buddies, both in my front yard and at the Dairy Queen. Forget the other two girls who had also filed reports with the police; I, his friend, had betrayed him.

That summer after my sophomore year, the candy coating of my happy life started to crack. I faced social rejection, a sixteen-year-old's worst fear. I confronted the illness and potential death of a child I loved. I grieved the end of a marriage and a family for the first time. I cried a lot and always at night, keeping my tears confined to the cab of my little pickup, where no one could see me.

I didn't have a place for my sadness. I thought that my bad feelings came from somewhere outside of me, reactions to situations I could fix if I tried harder, prayed more, or convinced the right people. And yet there I was, crying in my truck, thrust into an uncomfortable and yet familiar shadow, splitting myself into sun and moon. This darkness sang songs in my bones, and I didn't want it. It echoed deep within me, growing like a seed, like the final lines from Kloefkorn's poem:

The itch forever.
Of something small but ripening,
Underneath.

I pressed on into my junior year, turning my attention to a new group of friends who liked going to Bible class. A focus on God seemed to quash the new, dark feelings that had overwhelmed me the past summer. Weren't all teenagers filled with angst? If I kept up my happy persona and followed the rules of our subculture, I had both a ticket to eternal life and a way out of Seward: college. The rules were the Ten Commandments, the tenets of Luther's *Small Catechism*, and a host of behavioral standards passed down in word and deed by my parents and the St. John congregation at large. Here are six examples:

Rule #1: Be modest in behavior and dress. Wear turtlenecks and jumpers, avoid showing off your legs in short skirts, and wear a slip. You can wear makeup, but don't use too much color, go easy on the eyeliner, and lean toward pinks and plums for lips and nails.

Rule #2: Don't have sex until you are married. Don't talk about your sexuality outside of health or religion class, because knowledge is a slippery slope into the backseat of a young man's Chevy. I learned this at school, not at home. Ohlmanns do not talk about sex.

Rule #3: Pursue your talents, but don't be a diva. God gave you those gifts and he could easily take them away if you get too big for your britches.

Rule #4: Don't use foul language. "Suzanne," says my mother to this day, "there is always another more appropriate word available." I heard her say "Damnit!" once when I was a child, but it was because Dad had accidentally unplugged the deep freeze, which is the equivalent of Mom's Lost Ark of the Covenant, an act that could have spoiled the four hundred Cool Whip containers full of tomato sauce she faithfully made each August, along with a good pile of frozen meat from the quarter beef we'd split that winter with the Brauers, our next-door neighbors.

Rule #5: Don't discuss bodily functions. To acknowledge the body is to know the body, which can lead to sexual activity. I can still hear my dad admonishing me when I was five, after I'd dropped an audible fart. "Suzy, that is impolite. There are ways to pass gas in a manner that is both discreet and silent. At the very least, you should leave the room."

Rule #6: Go to church. Go to a Lutheran Church and school. Go to a Lutheran Church and school of the Missouri Synod, like the one in which you were raised, where they practice closed communion, or what I like to call "Members-Only Forgiveness," the body and blood of Jesus Christ and its redemptive properties saved for the select few who have discovered the precise means of eternal salvation—as opposed to all other Christian faiths, even other Lutherans, outside the synod. I am not making this up.

These rules didn't match the principles of teenage life in Seward. Church friends flashed me in jazz band, had sex in cornfields, farted audibly in study hall, and yelled "Shit!" when the soft-serve machine broke down at the Dairy Queen. I tried in earnest to walk the righteous walk, but even in the company of other rule-abiding friends, feelings of unworthiness followed me like a dark cloud. I had a sense that even if I did everything right, I'd never measure up.

I'd already failed the teenage social order, and as I recited the confession at the beginning of the liturgy every Sunday morning, I knew I was doomed.

*Most merciful God, we confess that we are by nature sinful and unclean.* (I already knew this because I came to Earth through a sinful act.) *We have* sinned against you in thought, word, and deed, by what we have done and by what we have left undone. (I'm pretty sure my deeds were acceptable on most days, especially in the sex category, as I'd all but frozen my body from the shoulders to the knees after years of sexual fear preached to me by my junior high religion teachers and life in a home where sex and the body were to be maintained in repressive silence.) We have not loved you with our whole heart. (How are we supposed to do that? I don't feel like I have a whole heart.) We have not loved our neighbors as ourselves. (Wait a minute. I love my neighbors. The Brauers are funny and kind, and they always let me use their basketball hoop. They often eat supper after seven o'clock, exotic in comparison with our five-thirty farm-time ritual. Larry Brauer is so unconventional that he sometimes does yard work in the dark. Is this all because they are Methodist?) We justly deserve your present and eternal punishment. (Does this mean things will actually get worse than they are in high school? Does anyone else in this church think life is awful as it is right now, or am I alone?) For the sake of your son Jesus Christ, have mercy on us. Forgive us (please), renew us (I'm thinking I need more repairing than just renewal, because what I actually feel is broken), and lead us, so that we may delight in your will (yes, about that: what am I supposed to do with my life?) and walk in your ways, to the glory of your holy name. Amen.

I don't know if it was God's will, but with each passing month of high school, my longing to find my biological family became less contained. An entry from my nightly journal on my seventeenth birthday, junior year, reads, "I wonder what my biological parents are feeling today. My heart yearns for them. I am alone in feeling."

My birth parents seemed a distant fairy tale during my early childhood, but as I grew into the age they had been when I was conceived, the lack of tangible information about them began to drive me mad. I had always been curious. When I was five, I told my babysitter, Esther, who transcribed many of our conversations onto note cards with the date and time, "You know what? I came out of a different woman's tummy."

When I was ten, my fourth grade teacher asked us to paint a picture of ourselves as adults doing our dream job. Mine featured me driving a red Ferrari across a tropical scene, just like Magnum PI. Most kids drew firefighters or ballplayers or ballerinas, but I wanted to become a private investigator because they knew how to find people.

My agitation only increased when I started playing in the Tri-City Youth Symphony, a high school group made up of kids from Grand Island, Kearney, and Hastings (and us stragglers from Seward) that rehearsed every Saturday morning at Grand Island Senior High School. Rehearsals required me to (1) give up my precious Saturday morning sleep-until-noon ritual and (2) drive to and from my birthplace every flipping week.

As a child I threw tantrums when our family stopped in Grand Island on our way west to Colorado to visit cousins. No one, including me, understood just why I reacted in this way. Then, when I was in fifth grade, my older brother started to play in the Tri-City Youth Symphony. One Saturday Mom and Dad decided we would drive him there ourselves and do some shopping at the Conestoga Mall while he rehearsed. In the end they were able to appease my tears with a pair of Jordache jeans and a new Michael Jordan windbreaker. Though I spent that morning at the mall scanning the crowds for my biological mother and father—I had no idea what they looked like, but I believed I would just know when I saw them that they were mine, just like they say you "just know" when you meet the person you're meant to marry—I ended the day with new memories to associate with Grand Island, and when I was old enough to play violin in the symphony myself, I did.

I also knew it would give me a chance to do some sleuthing. In the spring of junior year, a few weekends after my birthday, my violin stand partner and lifelong buddy Flora and I left rehearsal, downed lunch at Arby's, and headed to the Grand Island Public Library. We'd brainstormed for weeks all the ways we could uncover my past, but we only came up with one that was viable: high school yearbooks. If my birth mom was from Grand Island (and why wouldn't she be if I was born there?), she surely had attended high school. And thanks to my dad, we knew her first name, as he'd accidentally seen her signature on some paperwork at the time of my adoption.

"I don't believe I'm supposed to see this," Dad had told the social worker, Gary, who gasped and whisked the papers away. What Dad did not tell Gary, however, was that until that moment, he and Mom had planned to give me the same first name as my birth mother: Leah. Later, when I met Leah, I told her about this coincidence. She replied by saying she'd chosen Suzanne as my name before deciding to give me up.

Whenever I asked Dad to tell me my birth mother's full name, he'd claim he had purposely forgotten her last name so that I wouldn't be tempted to search for her until the appropriate time. "Curiosity killed the cat, Suzy," Dad reminded me, shaking his head over a pile of books. He'd set up a worktable in our basement TV room so we could spend time together watching our favorite shows, like *Falcon Crest* and *Carol Burnett and Friends*.

"Dad, come on," I cried, flailing around on the couch.

"Why don't we get out your file and take a look again?"

Dad's home office is the Ohlmann Family Vertical File, and thus I have access to artwork from fourth grade, programs from every music recital of my life, and all the documents they received throughout the adoption process. He pulled the folder from his desk drawer and handed me the one page, the birth profile, that calmed me when my yearning flared.

I pored over the information—my weight and length at birth, feeding schedule and formula, and characteristics of my parents: height, weight, hair color, eye color. Even with these spare attributes, I believed in my heart that these two people were beautiful and funny, and that, should we ever meet, they would fall in love with me.

At the Grand Island Public Library, Flora and I paged through stacks of high school yearbooks, but we came up empty. So in February of my senior year, a month before my eighteenth birthday, I sent a letter to Lutheran Family Services stating that the moment I crossed the threshold into adulthood, I wished to begin my search. Three weeks later, they replied.

LUTHERAN FAMILY AND SOCIAL SERVICE OF NEBRASKA, INC.

NAME OF CHILD __baby girl Ohlmann    Suzanne Elise Ohlmann__

BIRTHDATE __March 22nd, 1976__

PLACE OF BIRTH __Grand Island, Ne__      TIME __9:27 a.m.__

BIRTH WEIGHT: __7 lbs__

BIRTH LENGTH: __19½ inches__

MEASUREMENTS: ____ Head __13"__      Chest __13"__

APGAR: 1 minute __8½__    5 minutes __9__

FORMULA __Enfamil "20"__      FEEDING SCHEDULE __1½ to 2 oz - 4 hrs.__

## CHARACTERISTICS

| MOTHER | | FATHER |
|--------|---|--------|
| 21 yrs | AGE | 20 yrs |
| 5'9" | HEIGHT | 6'2" |
| 130 | WEIGHT | 150 |
| medium | BUILD | slender |
| green | EYE COLOR | green |
| brown | HAIR COLOR | light brown |
| medium | COLORING | light |
| high school | EDUCATION | 11th |
| art, painting | HOBBIES AND SKILLS | art |
| Swedish/German | NATIONALITY | |

MEDICAL HISTORY:

bio mother - good health          bio-father - asthma
            hay fever

COMMENTS:

pleasant personality, concerned about the welfare of her child.

1. Birth profile. Courtesy of the author.

Home alone, I ripped open the envelope and skimmed the crisp Courier font from a dot matrix printer, two pages packed with tight, single-spaced paragraphs. The letter was written in legalistic language sprinkled with therapeutic jargon, a tone that produced confusing sentences like this one: "The desire to search for birthparents can often be metaphorical." (What part is the metaphor? The search? The parents?) And this one: "Should the party you are searching for contact the agency after the paid time has been exhausted, we will negotiate with them their desires concerning contact and you will be billed for the extra time in making contact with that person or any follow-up with yourself." (I have to pay for follow-up with myself? Or with that person? Is that person my mom? And if so, I have to keep paying to contact her?)

I gave up on comprehension but absorbed the gist of the message: my name had been added to a search list. Once I reached the top, I'd hear from the Lutherans again, and after payment, the search would begin.

The dining room, the house, the western sun shining on Mom's dormant garden, all stood as they had before I'd opened the letter. But a shift rumbled through my inner landscape, new fault lines along an old chasm.

I crept into the kitchen to look through the back porch windows and make sure Mom and Dad weren't pulling into the driveway. Safe and alone, I crumpled to the floor. I'd never cried about my lost family. I didn't have rules to navigate this part of me. I had to get out of Seward.

# 4

# Archangel

I use the word "monster" to describe human beings whose shadows loom larger than anything else in their life and, in the end, destroy them. My birth dad, Mike, was a monster. I love and mourn him, but he was arrested multiple times for drunk driving, he wore an ankle bracelet in lieu of jail time (due to his asthma), he cheated on girlfriends and wives, he sired babies out of wedlock, and he spent his free time at a strip club drinking cheap beer. Mike's shadow loomed large and left wreckage in its wake.

I grew up around monsters disguised as people of Christian faith. They were the minority—just two men out of a host of attentive, loving teachers in our Lutheran church and school—but they were dynamic leaders who won awards both in our community and nationally for their brilliant teaching.

In my childhood bedroom, I'd go to sleep each night with my bedside lamp, a wall sconce, and my overhead light on, so afraid of the dark, of demons in the night who might take me away. But the monsters weren't in my house or lurking down the street. They were in my church, serving communion and teaching religion to children coming of age. They taught me to read fiction and to see light, contrast, and color in art. They taught me about sex and how wrong and sinful it was. They played videos about circumcision, about hell, about the elevators that took nonbelievers who drank and got in the backseats of boys' cars straight down to fiery damnation. These men lived publicly Lutheran lives. They drove minivans, kept clean lawns, piled their plates with casseroles at potlucks, gave my classmates nicknames, and made all of us feel special, important, and vital.

But they were monsters. They committed acts of sexual abuse on children at our sacred school and church, then donned robes and prayed the Prayers of the Church on Sunday mornings. I had two women teachers who taught me about sexuality in seventh and eighth grade health class, and they did so well and with a scientific and caring intention. One let us write down and submit questions anonymously, and then she answered them in open class discussion. (Mine was related to certain male organs knowing how to find certain female openings. With three options, how did the man's organ locate the correct destination, I wondered.)

But the monsters were the men, and in the Missouri Synod version of the Lutheran world, the men dominate. Women cannot be pastors, nor can they serve communion, read the Prayers of the Church, or serve as elders or presidents of congregations. If a problem arises in the church or school, it is primarily the men in leadership who hear about it, address it, and deal with it. So when children reported abuse to their mothers, the mothers reported this to a network of male leaders that included the monsters. Through eyes blinded by either faith, ignorance, or guilt, the leadership overlooked the children's reports. And in spite of the earnest teaching of all the women who taught me from kindergarten through ninth grade, it was the male voices that dominated my religious and sexual education, particularly during my adolescent years and concurrent confirmation training.

As an innocent servant child, I admired my male teachers, but as an adult, I feel like they've taken a vat of liquid pig feces and dumped it over my head. I wash and wash, but I never lose the stench. Though beloved, award-winning teachers, they were monsters, and their shadows loom over my childhood memories. I remember music from school, I perceive beauty in the art and literature I studied there, but then comes the next sense: the sour taste of bile on my tongue.

Then again, I arrived in Seward and joined my happy Lutheran family with the taste of bile in my mouth. I was placed days late in my parents' home because I'd been crying, vomiting, struggling to eat, and struggling to poop. It's as if my tiny self knew I'd come from a monster's world and I wanted to go back. Monsters were my people. But poverty and unwanted pregnancies—addiction, illicit drug use, and sex with multiple partners—don't mix with Luther's *Small Catechism* and the glorious pageantry of the Christmas Eve services of my childhood. Those behaviors lived outside the bounds of my new community . . . or so we were told.

But they lived within me, in my cells. After growing up with hopes of fulfilling the ideals of my adopted realm, after a childhood of proving myself to the "clean living" folks of my idyllic small town, I launched into the real world with my own shadow looming. After Lutheran college, a failed attempt at grad school, and a broken off engagement to my loving college sweetheart, my sense of self—though clear enough to break promises—ached like an open wound, weeping with shame. To reinforce my self-loathing, I sought intimacy in the arms of men who were unavailable at best and at worst, abusive.

Enter Ariel, a muscular, tattooed, motorcycle-riding Costa Rican working under a fake social security number. He was both sexy and a sociopath, the perfect attraction and punishment for a repressed Nebraskan girl wracked with guilt for breaking her fiancé's heart and, worse, leaving the path of righteousness.

We met in Minneapolis at First Avenue's weekly Salsa Inferno dance night, me twenty-three, lean, in a bright, flowery summer dress and Ariel, nearly thirty, broad, tan, and striking in a white guayabera with flames stitched into the embroidery.

I saw him watching me dance, his expression that of a hunter: lupine eyes, arched brows, looking like Benicio del Toro had been cast as the vampire Lestat. He was taller than most of my dance partners, and during one of my favorite salsas, "Brujería (Witchcraft)" by El Gran Combo, he cut in, led me up the stairs to a corner of the stage, and cast his spell.

"I've been watching you," he said.

Every inch of my skin swelled with heat. I'd lost my virginity to my fiancé, but this felt like an immersion baptism. I had been taught to *never* feel this good.

Ariel grasped the sides of my rib cage, then my hips, and forced my body's energy from my shoulders to my core, my *cadera*. We danced and he held me close, so close, his breath on my neck, my mouth at his ear. I took the nub of his earlobe in my teeth and gave it a playful tug. Who had I just become? He squeezed my hips and lifted me off my feet, his mouth on my neck, while El Gran Combo sang the chorus:

*Tú me hiciste brujería!*
*BRRRR! Demonio!*

You cast a spell on me!
BRRRR! Demon!

I had no defense for the machinations of this *demonio* Ariel. The restrictive sex teachings of the Christian monsters never addressed the fact that I would be so deeply attracted to a man who would cause me such pain. The repression of sexuality, the all-out condemnation of its presence in the way I was acculturated, left me fumbling in a sea of ignorance and with zero self-respect when it came to my body. I could only respond to praise and my foreign, forbidden instincts. Any insult or abuse felt familiar, even expected, since I was ashamed of being a sexual being in the first place—sexual outside the confines of Christian marriage, that is, and worse, in a public place and on a stage that once had cradled the incarnation of sex himself, Prince! This, plus my baseline of self-loathing, or as Roy Blount Jr. calls it, "sefflo," set me up for victimization and addictive behavior—seeking the high of admiration, attention, and infatuation in spite of the profound lows that were to follow.

After our first night of dancing, Ariel began visiting me at my coffee shop job for a quick kiss and free chocolate cake. He took me to Latin

American restaurants and taught me the aphrodisiac powers of food. His favorite dish, *sopa de siete mares*, was a rich seafood stew with seven different kinds of fish and shellfish, all said to embolden the libido. I'm not sure he needed the help, but I relished our "lessons." Aphrodisiacs were never mentioned at any point in my upbringing, unless you consider Jell-O or Cool Whip to arouse the senses.

Ariel so quickly broadened my world, making me smell and taste and climax in ways I'd never known, that I barely noticed the shift in his behavior. What had begun as encouragement and excitement at my attempt to speak Spanish with him became belittling, then blatant laughter at my mistakes. He began doing this in front of other bilingual friends or speaking to them about me in idiomatic phrases I didn't understand. What started as constant praise of my body became stinging insults about my style of underpants or how I shaved my legs and sacred midlands.

"I feel like he wants me to look like a porn star," I said to a friend, even before Ariel and I started having sex.

These were warnings of things to come, but I ignored them, so hungry for his approval, so sure that he would come to appreciate me the way he had in the beginning and that I would again feel like I had on the stage at First Avenue.

I didn't tell my parents about the salsa dancing, or Ariel, or the duffle bag of porn and guns and cocaine he'd asked me to keep for him while his dad visited from Costa Rica. The guy had BAD IDEA written all over him, but for six months I whirled through his vortex, explaining away his mood swings to friends, pretending he wasn't occasionally shoving me into walls. The first time he raped me, we'd gone for a run together and come back to his apartment to shower and eat lunch. He'd complimented me on our jog, how good my body looked in the purple sports bra and running shorts I'd worn, making special note of the fact that the running shorts precluded any need for underwear. I ignored the comments, unaware of his plans to force himself inside me once we arrived home and he could hold me down on the bed. And afterward, when I stumbled into the shower, he pulled a kitchen chair into the bathroom, ripped the shower curtain open, and watched.

He was an abuser and I his victim, caught in the classic cycle of victimization. One solid, peaceful evening together, enjoying our favorite Chinese takeout and snuggling with a movie, bought him days of erratic, violent behavior. My arms and thighs became checkered with bruises. I wasn't his only girlfriend either. I caught the voices of other women on his answering machine, and friends spotted him out with different dance partners on nights I worked. When I'd confront him, he'd curl his fingers around my neck in a choking position and then lean in for a kiss. When we'd go out with my college friends, he'd keep his hand under the table and dig his fingernails into the skin of my thigh. He'd study my reaction to the pain with a smirk, pause, and then squeeze harder until tears sprang to my eyes, my only option being to smile and pretend I was choking on something. I'd paired up with a monster, my own personal Hades, to drag me down into the underworld and confirm once and for all that I had escaped from the Light and, thanks to Ariel, fallen straight into the Darkness.

But then he got deported, and I went to Planned Parenthood and got tested for everything: negative. I saw a therapist at the Chrysalis Center for Women. I moved through life like a shell for months, scared to be alone with any man, even my own dad, Glenn, gentlest of men. Aside from the constant voice of judgment in my head droning "you should have known better," I wept, knowing I'd trusted Ariel and Ariel alone with my biggest secret: that I knew I couldn't marry anyone or truly become an adult until I found my biological family. I couldn't admit that to my (now ex-) fiancé, my girlfriends, or my parents, but of all the people in my life, I'd chosen a monster to hold my story, and he had.

I met Ariel just months after I'd tracked down my birth mother's address and phone number in Nebraska and drummed up the courage to write her a letter. The same week I dove into the Salsa Inferno and met Ariel, she'd written me back a handwritten letter in black ballpoint ink and a girlish cursive script.

She wrote how glad she was to hear from me and that she'd tried a thousand times to put her thoughts into words. Like me, she'd struggled to find the right things to say, so for years she'd said nothing. And she'd kept me a secret from her husband and her kids—her six other children.

She worried about how our communication would affect my parents, and she thanked them for all they'd done for me. (Here I alternated between feeling awkward and feeling elated; of course my parents deserved thanks, but I didn't want to be her messenger.)

Just home from the late shift at a factory, she apologized that her exhaustion made her ramble. *Do ramble, my lovely, lost mom,* I thought. *Please keep rambling until, say, the second coming of Christ or the arrival of the Four Horsemen or the sound of the last Trumpet.*

With continued self-deprecation, she apologized for her poor letter writing skills and that she couldn't give me more details. She'd fill me in on my siblings later. I wouldn't have to wait as long for her to write next time, she promised.

She closed by saying she had always loved me very much. *Always,* I thought. *The gutting, the sucker punch of abandonment, and she'd loved me.*

I kept the letter by my bed and committed it to memory. I had six siblings! When I shared the news with my parents, they expressed their support for the connection.

"Well, now we know that you are fecund," Mom said.

I had to look up *fecund* in the dictionary. I thought it meant *poop*.

Days after we'd met, I told Ariel about my birth mother and read him her letter. He pulled me onto his lap and I cried. I felt like he'd come to my life for this exact reason—a stranger who grasped the strangeness in me. On the good nights, when he acted like a normal person, even a friend, he asked me about her and would say, repeatedly, "Call her. You need her. She needs you."

Once immigration sent Ariel packing, I moved apartments and worked multiple jobs to save money to move to New York. I kept salsa dancing, lived in a studio apartment in the Wedge neighborhood, and navigated the Twin Cities without a car for over a year. Just months before I planned to move, in the summer of 2001, I thought I saw Ariel jogging in my neighborhood.

That weekend, as I twirled away with a harmless dance partner, my friend Jess grabbed me by the elbow and guided me to the bathroom with notable speed.

"He's here," she said.

Cathy, the third member of our salsa trio, joined us, her face pale, eyes wide.

They recruited some friends and formed a circle around me like the Secret Service. We left out the back.

"He saw you," Jess said.

I went home and threw up.

The next week Ariel left a note at my job. He'd had a near-death experience while surfing in Costa Rica, and his out-of-body experience included a beatific vision of me and the realization he'd made a mistake. I struggle to imagine that I was the only "mistake" that appeared during this miracle, but I digress. I'd like to say that I took the letter, burned it, moved to New York, and never gave that toxic dickweed another thought, that I was emboldened by my trauma, had learned appropriate boundaries, and never wanted to see him again.

Instead I called the number he'd left on the note and asked him if he wanted some of the books he'd left with me when he got deported. That's right, a good librarian's daughter, I'd kept his bloody books, probably in alphabetical order by author's last name. I apologized for the fact that the motorcycle he'd left on my curb was no longer in my possession, despite the repeated, chilling threats he'd left on my voicemail from an unreachable international number soon after his government-sponsored departure.

"They impounded it when it snowed, so the plows could get through," I said. "Sorry."

These choices mortify me to this day: a boyfriend beat and raped me, and when he returned, I fell for his near-death experience, drove a box of books to his new apartment, and within minutes, lay flat on my back as he rammed my shoulders into the mattress.

"I could do it again, Suz."

I nodded.

For some reason, he jumped off and made some Café Bustelo coffee.

"You ever call your mom?"

I shook my head.

He stirred sugar into my cup and slid it across the table.

"You're starving, Suzanita. You must be so hungry for your family."

*Can the Buddha inhabit a sociopath who makes amazing coffee?* I wondered.

I left intact and, days later, moved to New York.

That Christmas, 2001, I finally found the courage to call my birth mother. I was flying home to Nebraska, safe in the anonymity of LaGuardia Airport and its heightened security in the wake of September 11. Any residual trauma from Ariel's abuse, along with my primal fears of Leah's rejection, paled in comparison to the alarming new norms of New York life, including armed guards with AR-15's greeting me each morning at the Ninety-Sixth Street subway station.

As I stood in line at security, I heard a TSA announcement about the new shoe removal protocol. *Fudge*, I thought. *My socks.* I'd overslept my alarm that morning, and in the rush to pack and then catch my cab, I'd discovered I was out of clean socks and I'd thrown on a dirty pair of moth-eaten footies from the bowels of my closet. The comic element of exposing my swiss-cheese socks to the lines of strangers surrounding me, let alone the highly inspectorial security guards, destroyed any shred of personal dignity I'd brought to the airport in the wee hours and somehow led to a sense of liberation from my pre-9/11 fears about almost everything, including contacting my birth mother. What did I have to lose?

So I called from the gate area. She answered. I was over-caffeinated and sleep deprived, and I have no memory of the words we exchanged. But I can still hear the ring of her voice—so polite and melodic—and feel the catch in my own, like a hand just placed at the base of my neck.

I've come to understand that people in abusive relationships aren't having a rational experience; they're responding to an unhealthy attraction, to inertia, and many times, to love. My choices seemed poor and, to me, inevitable, but now that I understand more of the psychology of being victimized, I can forgive myself and sometimes forgive Ariel and the other monsters in my past. I confess I'm still curious about my abuser. I wonder what ways he's found to self-destruct and to torture other women in the last twenty years. I hope I never know.

I wouldn't say I feel gratitude toward Ariel, but I wouldn't have called my birth mother without his support and urging. He was the first person to truly empathize with the pain my buried past caused me. Maybe the only reason I confided in him was because I felt safe revealing my skeletons to a monster. At age twenty-three, unable to keep my promise to get married and live according to my parents' ideals, I felt like an ungrateful daughter and a failed member of my adopted tribe. I teetered on the cusp of my own underworld, and Ariel's abuse both pushed me over the edge and, somehow, proved I could survive the darkness.

# 5

## Mom versus the Addict

Until I was in my midthirties, I made a habit of climbing on top of my mother at bedtime during my visits home to Nebraska. She'd lie there in the light of her bedside lamp, covers up to her chest, editorial page of the *Omaha World-Herald* in hand, my dad next to her, nose buried in his current novel or biography. I'd stand at the foot of the bed and wait for the collective groan before I began my ascent. They knew the drill.

"Mommy," I'd say as I snuggled my head on her chest.

"Good grief," she'd chuckle, a touch winded from my adult body weight. Unable to continue reading, she'd hold the paper aside with one hand and pat my back with the other.

I think Dad knew this was a strange habit for a grown woman. We all knew. I'd gone to great lengths to put distance between my mother and me, living each phase of my life farther and farther from Nebraska. When I was home to visit, she and I could clear the room with a cocktail of tension, verbal or not, mixed from a long list of recurring conflicts. And yet each night you'd find me there, a five-foot, eight-inch, 150-pound baby.

Mom grew up in Columbus, Nebraska, an hour northwest of Seward, raised mostly by her grandma Ahrens while her mom worked at the Safeway grocery store and her dad ran several service stations. Ninety-six Union Pacific Railroad trains a day passed just a block and a half from

Mom's childhood home on the corner of Fourteenth Avenue and Fourteenth Street, the place I came to know as Grandma and Grandpa A's, a small house with sage green siding, white trim, and a front porch swing.

When Grandpa's family lost the farm in the Great Depression and moved to town, he and his father worked as day laborers, scooping coal off those same trains to support their growing family. When he joined the navy in March of 1944 and deployed to the Pacific theater of World War II, the trains brought him home on leave to the depot downtown, and he'd walk the mile back to their house. He loved to tell the story of how one time he knocked at the front door, unaware that Grandma was doing wash in the basement and couldn't hear him, and his two little ones, overrun with excitement at the sight of their daddy, couldn't figure out how to unlock the door. "Patty yanking away on the knob, and Bob turning around in circles."

Now I live close to trains in San Antonio, just three blocks from tracks that form the eastern and southern perimeters of the neighborhood, train whistles coloring the soundscape of life the way they did for my mother growing up and for me on all my visits to Grandma and Grandpa's house. I might be washing dishes or filling the bird feeder in the yard, but when a train whistle sounds, I'm back in Columbus, mashing potatoes with Grandma in the kitchen or playing Polish rummy at the dining room table with Grandpa, his lips pursed and eyes twinkling as he lays down his hand in a methodical show of dominance.

I didn't notice the trains the day I visited the house with my real estate agent and decided to make an offer. Several years before, the city of San Antonio had redone the street, paved new sidewalks, and buried all the power lines. An artist, Anne Wallace, had collected stories from the neighborhood's multigenerational inhabitants and pressed excerpts of their narratives into the freshly poured cement. Anne's installation turned my street into a book of poems. Just outside the front gate at my house, the sidewalk reads, "We always lived close to a train for some strange reason."

My mother loves to read, and on her first visit to my house, she took to the sidewalks to read all of Anne Wallace's inscriptions. She leans more toward prose than poetry, both in reading material and worldview. She appreciated the words on my front walk and even connected them with Grandma and Grandpa's house, though we both know I'm more nostalgic about trains, and everything else, than she is. She's a planner and a doer. If an artist were to inscribe a message on her front sidewalk, it would read, "Be appropriate."

My mother thrives on routine. She keeps multiple lists of plans and tasks, and is happy to delegate when necessary to fulfill her plans. When Grandma A died, the family gathered at my parents' house the day before the funeral. Mom entered the living room with a stack of index cards, a task written on each one, and handed them out to us. They varied from "fill glasses with ice before dinner," to "prepare salad for today's lunch," to "go to funeral home to ensure Grandma looks appropriate."

After the funeral, we gathered again at my parents' for the evening meal. Mom fried some breakfast sausages and whipped up a batch of Bisquick pancakes, a simple supper after a long day. We ate and shared stories around the table, all of us in disbelief that we'd actually buried Grandma that afternoon. As the meal progressed, Mom had her mind on food, not memories, and noted a distinct lack of second servings.

"I presume some of you would like more pancakes?" she asked.

We all agreed.

"Before I make more, I want to be *sure* that you will eat the entire batch."

A collective gulp sounded from around the table, all of us now unsure about our level of commitment to the pancakes.

"Go ahead, Mom," I said.

She stood to go to the kitchen, eyebrows raised, waving her index finger like a math teacher to a rowdy class.

As the conversation relaxed back to Grandma stories, I heard Mom's whisk and the sound of Pam spraying into the electric frying pan. But as the minutes passed, my aunt, then my cousin, then Dad, then all of us decided that maybe we didn't need that second batch after all. We discussed our options in hushed tones.

"But how are we going to tell Pat?"

"You tell her. I'm not going to."

"We'd better not—let's just eat them."

"Oh, come on, it's just pancake mix."

"Yes, but it's *Pat*."

"I'll tell her. It's okay," my cousin Katie volunteered.

Silence fell over the table as she tiptoed into the kitchen.

"Pat?" she asked.

A pause.

"You are going to eat them!" Mom roared.

We ate every last one.

My mother plays by the rules and feels compelled to remind me when I don't. She sees the world in black and white, and I live in gray. Several years ago I flew to Nebraska for our hometown's annual Fourth of July celebration, the day culminating in a parade down the old, red bricks of Seward Street. Thousands lined the route, having staked their place with blankets and lawn chairs that they set up in the days before. I stood in our family's annual spot and laughed at the parade's antics: local politicians walking and waving as they tossed Tootsie Rolls and Jolly Ranchers to the crowd; polka bands serenading Czech Queens and Pork Queens and Rodeo Queens from the back of tractor trailers; old farmers driving antique tractors, dressed in Key overalls and DeKalb caps; the Seward High School Band marching past, looking younger every year.

A classmate from both grade school and high school, Mike, hollered my name. His family was camped next to ours, though I hadn't noticed. This was Mike, whose family owned the liquor store on the highway coming into town and who in first grade wore chunky brown shoes that I called "little loaves of bread" on the playground, which infuriated Mike, which made him tattle on me, which made me have to stay inside for the next recess. He found revenge by calling me Plywood throughout junior high, apparently due to my flat chest. I was happy to see him now and even happier when he offered me a can of Busch Light, the beer of choice in Seward County.

We tucked our beers into koozies, toasted our shared memories, and threw back a couple of swigs.

"Ahem," my mother said, clearing her throat.

"Mom—you remember Mike, right?"

Mike reached out his hand to shake Mom's.

"Yes, hello, Michael," she said quickly, seeming annoyed with the gesture. "You two do realize it is illegal to drink from an open container in public?"

"Mom," I said, "it's the Fourth of July."

"That may be, Suzanne, but—"

"Miss Ohlmann?" Mike interrupted her. "With all due respect, me and Suzy here? We're grown."

Beer shot out of my nose, though Mike's candor was not altogether unexpected. But when Mom speaks in teacher voice, her authoritative tone is the kind that few people outside of our immediate family dare to challenge. A teaching colleague of Mom's once told me how greatly she appreciated Mom's assertive style in staff meetings. "Things go a lot quicker when your mom's there. We all just wait for her to shut up the people who blather on and then summarize things so we can go home. You know Pat—she doesn't take any guff."

Mom's pious expression remained while Mike, totally unfazed, stepped away to grab me a napkin. He was right when he said "grown." We had both turned thirty-five that year.

"Well," Mom said, "consider your 'grown selves' informed." And she returned to her lawn chair.

"Here you go, Suzy." Mike handed me a napkin. "You want another beer?"

I declined, not out of deference to Mom, but because Busch Light gives me gas. Mike's comment to my mother shook me up and laid bare a simple truth: I was grown. I was headed for middle age. Though it seemed I had carved my own path through life, and I had—childhood in Seward, music study at St. Olaf, singing and arts administration in New York, then nursing school, rural India, and finally San Antonio, where I had a good job, a permanent address, and a mortgage, for God's sake!—Mom's frequent admonitions triggered more than just beer spewing out of my nose. I felt ashamed and believed that I had disappointed her, that I would always disappoint her.

Three short months after the Busch Light Debacle at the Fourth of July parade, my parents came to visit me in San Antonio. I hadn't told them, but I was having trouble getting out of bed again, sure I was sliding into the sinkhole of another depression. Anxiety and depression for me were like the clouds of dust that followed Pigpen in the Peanuts cartoons. While Pigpen explained his dirty shadow as "the dust of countless ages," I was ashamed of my clouds. I didn't comprehend their origins.

On a beautiful fall morning, with a full day planned of cooking and home improvements, Mom and I decided to walk my dog, Pablo, through the neighborhood. Mom hoped to find more Anne Wallace sidewalk inscriptions.

Toward the end of our route, as we looked to cross South Presa Street toward the Taco Haven restaurant, a little white dog appeared a half block away on our side of the street. Noting our choice to cross, he set a diagonal course to meet us on the other side of Presa, oblivious to traffic. A Mack truck roared toward him. Pablo barked a warning bellow at the little white puff, I waved down the truck, and my mother took my elbow to hurry me across the street.

We made it to the corner and the little dog met us there, sniffed Pablo's nose, then his butt, then his under parts. He looked like a West Highland White Terrier, or Westie, but skinny, his ribs showing. I squatted down and let him sniff my hand.

"Suzanne—don't," Mom said.

She knows me. She knows my affection for animals, especially abandoned ones. She knows I got Pablo from the pound, along with my two cats back at the house. She knows that just one month before this white doglet showed up, I rescued a black lab puppy from the dog park, where he was dumped on September 11, and found him a new family. What kind of jerk dumps a dog on 9/11? Or ever?

Mom and I have always had different ideas of risk, she being risk-averse and I on the risk-prone end of the spectrum. Both traits have merit. For instance, when I was five years old and we were on a family vacation in the Black Hills, I decided I would enter and exit our Dodge station wagon Dukes of Hazzard style: through the window. Mom quickly put that habit to rest by making me sit in the car with her while Jeff and Dad went and toured Cosmos, a mystery museum.

Mom has lived the majority of her life within sixty miles of Columbus, Nebraska, where she was born. I've lived in multiple time zones and cultures, and I have a knack for arriving at my new digs in the midst of cataclysmic disaster. I moved to New York on August 28, 2001, just two weeks before 9/11. I flew into the east coast of India as the tsunami of December 26, 2004, hit. I moved to San Antonio after doing disaster work there in the midst of Hurricane Ike in September 2008.

My life in New York seemed particularly confounding to Mom. Several months after I arrived, I went to a concert at Lincoln Center that combined the Jazz at Lincoln Center house band with Tito Puente's salsa band (though Puente had died the year before). As I walked to get the train home afterward, I saw the bass player from Puente's band leaning against what was then Avery Fisher Hall.

"Tocaste como un angel," I told him. *You played like an angel.*

He thanked me, and as we chatted, the entire rhythm section appeared. They invited me to accompany them downtown that night to hear one of the Fania All-Stars, Cheo Feliciano, play at a club called S.O.B.'s. I checked my gut, felt a green light, and hopped in a van with my new friends. As we cruised down Ninth Avenue, they were speaking Spanglish and ranting about how a combo tune they'd just performed with the Jazz at Lincoln Center band had nearly derailed.

"Sabias?" they asked me. *Could you tell?*

"Sabia que?" I asked. *Could I tell what?*

"That we nearly shit the bed on stage?" the bass player laughed.

This is why I'd moved to New York: to be with musicians, to make connections, to hop in a van with a bunch of salseros and drive downtown to hear Cheo Feliciano.

This would never have happened to my mother—not the location, not the language, not the genre of music—and I would never have told her about that wonderful night of music and newfound friendship. I once brought her to see a salsa band I followed in Minneapolis, and I can still see her in her black turtleneck, gray tweed blazer, and sterling silver cross pendant, her fingers plugged into her ears.

We may have different views on risk, but I believe we both have lived solid, respectable lives. Mom knows this about me. She also knows that I am approaching middle age. I own my own home and have college degrees from two fine institutions. I've traveled the world and learned to speak several languages, and I have a strong credit score. Yet none of this seemed to register when I approached the white doggy with the wagging tail.

"Mom, please," I groaned as I rose to my feet.

"I am just telling you, Suzanne, do *not* take this dog home."

I stomped my foot.

Pablo and the white dog commenced playing right there on the corner, bowing and jumping as if they were long lost friends who had planned this reunion for months.

We started walking.

The dogs walked side by side, Pablo an eighty-five pound German shepherd mix, the little white dude a quarter of Pabber's weight and malnourished, his white coat grayed from the street. When we stopped again and I leaned down to assess his overall health, I found a pink, baseball-sized wound on his left flank. His teeth were black. I noticed this because every time I bent down, he smiled up at me, his scraggy tail twirling like a helicopter.

I swear he was saying, "Hi, Mom!"

I swear Pablo was saying, "Keep smiling, brother. She's stocked with peanut butter and there's a ton of squirrels in the yard."

Every time the white dog smiled, my mother sighed and shook her head.

We started to walk again. For half a block, I wondered if the white dog might not split off from us and follow the smell of an errant squirrel. But no. He walked the rest of the way at Pablo's side, turned into the driveway like he'd done it a million times, and dashed into the yard as soon as I opened the gate.

"Why, there's a cute little white doggy!" my dad said as he tinkered with the back porch screen Pablo had blown out the day before. (Though the possum escaped, I don't think he'll be returning anytime soon.)

"Isn't he cute, Dad? I feel like he and Pablo are old friends. Not quite sure what to do, but I couldn't let him starve on the street."

"Nope, Glenn, she couldn't. Not our daughter. Not Suzanne," Mom said, heading up the back steps into the house. The door shut thwack! behind her.

Dad pounded another nail into the screen frame.

I watched the dogs play and tried to breathe, my chest tight from the brief but effective shame storm. Why was my soft spot for animals so frustrating to my mother? I'd invited my parents for a visit to my house, a place I loved, a home that was made perfect by the trains. She'd sat and drunk coffee with me in the quiet breeze on the front porch that morning, listening to stories of my steady-paycheck nursing job. Like Grandpa A in a game of Polish rummy, I'd laid out my hand for her, the cards showing a stable, organized life; no trips to the ER for a drug overdose, no babies out of wedlock, no unkempt boyfriends farting at Thanksgiving dinner.

Pablo and his new friend scampered through the backyard in figure eights, like ballroom dancers separated for years, dusting off the old routine. Maybe I could learn some new choreography from these good dogs. Their grace and affection as they circled the yard made me wonder if I might need to change my routine with Mom. I wanted to blame her for the shame and "sefflo" she triggered, but Pablo and Little White Puff reminded me otherwise: it takes two to tango, and I had to quit the dance.

I needed the structure and organizational model my mother provided throughout childhood (and well into my thirties), but I have never known how to abide by Mom's rules completely. I shudder to consider the opportunities and relationships I might have missed had I adopted her worldview.

Had I followed the "Be appropriate" route, I would have abandoned that little white dog on the street, not out of malice but out of pragmatism. I would have muted the voice that whispered "This is your house" when I first stepped onto what became my front porch here in San Antonio, because the house would have seemed to be too old and too much work for a single woman on a nurse's salary. I would have missed Cheo Feliciano at S.O.B.'s. And years before settling down in San Antonio, halfway through nursing school at Columbia, I would have skipped the life-changing conversation I had with a psychiatric patient, because in order to convince the patient to talk to me, I had to break the rules. *Inappropriate.*

It was the exchange with my patient that had convinced me to seek out my birth mother again. I had given up on finding her, and for good reason. Two years before nursing school, on one of my long visits home to Nebraska, we set up our first reunion and she no-showed. After multiple conversations, she suggested the location, date, and time and then chose not to come. No call, no explanation, no effort to reschedule. She simply stood me up. I was twenty-nine.

Two years later, halfway through my psychiatric nursing rotation, I was assigned a "unique" patient, to use the social worker's word—a patient who refused to talk to anyone. Our clinical group had been working at a substance abuse inpatient rehabilitation facility just up the Hudson from New York. I was thirty-one and had no idea I was just a month and a half away from meeting my birth mother for the first time—this time for real.

"We want to provide some insight into Josh," said Elliot, the unit director and social worker, folding his arms across his chest. A recovering addict himself, Elliot conveyed both concern and reserve, even reticence, when it came to his patients. He spoke with a calm, deep voice and could have been the stunt double for Sam Shepard in *The Right Stuff*. "He's a unique patient, not that all our patients aren't unique, but Josh is particular at this time."

"Particular?" I asked. I tried to ingest Elliot's words there in the staff lounge, but I became hopelessly distracted because he bore such a striking resemblance to Sam Shepard, the actor, playwright, and former husband of Jessica Lange. When I was twenty-three, I had fantasized—in Sam and Jessica's presence as I served them cake at the cafeteria-style restaurant where I worked in St. Paul, Minnesota—that they had traveled over years and miles to my dessert station because they were my birth parents. It wasn't totally inconceivable, as Jessica and I had similar coloring and my biological father was surely a tall, lanky type like Sam, based on the height and weight listed for him in my birth profile. Why wouldn't my father also have a rugged smile, a Pulitzer Prize, and crow's feet that crinkled into handsome perfection around his mysterious yet welcoming eyes?

Elliot continued. "Josh refuses to talk to anyone. I've worked with him during his prior inpatient admissions, so he talks to me, but barely. Seems he'd prefer to remain a stranger to himself, and this is the last time his insurance will cover treatment."

"And he's a physician, right?" I asked.

"Yes, and about to lose his license, so he doesn't want to talk to nursing students, or anyone. Just keeps saying, 'You won't understand, you won't understand,' on and on."

I wondered why he'd decided to trust me with Josh. It could have been a random choice, but I'm not sure I believe in random. Elliot's intuition was rooted in years of addiction, followed by more years of sobriety, followed by turning back to fellow addicts to give them a hand out of the pit. He sensed the beasts rooted deep in my cells and that I might connect with Josh and make him feel secure and unjudged. Elliot knew, but I didn't, and so I stood there, blank.

"Listen, kid, go in there and do what you've been doing with all the other patients. You've got your questionnaire. Start with question one and see if he'll give you some answers."

I shrugged.

"You'll be fine. Just remember the rules of the caregiver in the psychiatric setting: your role is to listen. You ask the questions. Don't let him turn the tables on you, and never answer any personal questions."

"Okay," I sighed, sliding the chart into my bag.

I opened the door to leave and looked back at my mentor, smiling at me like a proud dad at a school bus stop. "Thanks, Elliot."

"He's in room seven. I'll check on you in thirty minutes."

I walked into the hall, noting its wan yellow cinder blocks, fluorescent lighting, and tired, speckled linoleum. Room seven was on my left, three doors down from the lounge. I set my bag outside the room and bent to touch my toes, heaving out an exhale. I was scared to meet Josh. He had twenty years of addiction on his back, his career at stake, and his insurance out of coverage, and he refused to talk. What could I possibly have to offer?

I straightened my clothes: pressed, white oxford, black, wrap-around cardigan, houndstooth pants. This was the one rotation for which we dressed professionally rather than in scrubs. I retied the ponytail at the back of my neck. I had no idea what I was doing.

"Be appropriate, Suzanne," my mother advised in my head.

"Start with question one," I heard Elliot's voice say.

After a long stare at the door, I knocked and peeked my head in. Josh sat with his arms crossed, staring down at the floor, an empty chair across from him. The room looked like a classroom, with desk chairs pushed to the sides and an overhead projector in the corner. His youth and clean-cut appearance surprised me, his dress similar to mine: black, cable-knit sweater over charcoal, tailored dress pants, polished loafers, and gray argyle socks.

"Mind if I sit down?" I gestured toward the empty chair.

He looked up at me through tortoise-shell glasses. A shock of brown, wavy hair cut across the smooth skin of his forehead.

"I don't care."

I sat down, pulling his chart from my bag to recheck his age. Thirty-nine, and he looked ten years younger than that.

"I'm not talking to anyone." He stared at his shoes.

"I heard."

"Anyone," he repeated, this time looking at me.

I decided to buy some time. I pulled out my legal pad and pen and gave Josh my most ponderous, clinical assessment gaze. I took a deep, analytical breath and wrote my name and date in the upper right-hand corner. I then began numbering down the page as if preparing for a fifth-grade spelling test. Occasionally I glanced up at Josh; then I wrote more numbers, my gestures swift and pointed.

"What are you writing?" he asked.

I knew he was watching me.

"You really want to know?" I kept my head down until I reached the bottom of the page, then turned the pad toward him. "Absolutely nothing."

He let out a half-chuckle and recrossed his legs.

The room felt stagnant, his refusal to connect creating a lumpy weight in the air. I needed to move around and free up the vibe, to initiate some kind of communication, even if I ended up talking to myself for the next fifty minutes. I started pacing and babbling, told him my name, how far along I was in nursing school, and how much longer we'd be doing clinicals on the unit, and I outlined the assignment questionnaire I'd hoped to complete with him that day. The whole while I felt silly, like a fledgling stand-up comic with a heckler my only audience, but the few times our eyes met, his eyebrows flinched with a hint of concern, even interest.

"Elliot's coming in to check on us soon." I stopped and gripped the back of my chair. "Will you at least tell me why you won't talk? Please?"

He adjusted his glasses and looked at me for a moment, blinking like a cat. "I'm not talking to anyone because I'm adopted."

Time shifted to slow motion as I slid around the front of the chair in an attempt to return to a seated position, my movements awkward, almost slithering, like I'd forgotten how to keep myself vertical.

"Say that again, Josh?"

"I said I'm not talking to anyone because I'm adopted. No one understands in this shithole because they all grew up with their biological families. You won't either, so why bother?"

"Oh," I coughed, my mouth too dry to speak or swallow. Tiny fountains of sweat spouted at the back of my neck as I tried to convey a sense of composure. I couldn't lie to Josh, but I wasn't supposed to tell the truth either. There he was, clearly suffering, his life a mess, and he was pinning the whole ordeal on the fact that he was adopted. I couldn't ignore the strict rules about communication with psychiatric patients, but Josh didn't feel like a psych patient anymore.

"Hey, what was your name again?" Josh leaned toward me. "You don't look so good. Do you need some air?"

"I'm fine," I said, dabbing a tissue over my face. "My name's Suzanne, and I'm adopted too."

"What?"

"I'm adopted. I get it."

Then Josh stood up and began pacing the room, running his hands through his hair. "I can't believe this. I can't believe this." He bounced from wall to wall. "This changes everything. When did you know? Have you met your birth parents? We have so much to talk about."

"Oh, God," I said. "It's such a long story."

"I want to hear it!" He jumped back into his chair and scooted close. "We can help each other. Tell me about your birth mom. Have you met her?"

I blushed.

"Knock-knock." Elliot stepped into the room. "How's everybody doing in here?"

"Elliot," Josh nodded. "Hey! We are doing good."

"Able to get to the assignment, Suzanne?" Elliot asked.

"Not yet, but—," I started.

"But we were just getting to it." Josh finished my sentence.

"You were just getting to it, were you, Josh?" Elliot seemed both aware of and entertained by our improvisation.

"Yes, we were. I like working with Suzanne. She's a good communicator."

Dear God. More blushing.

"Well, all right then, I'll get out of here so you can keep working. Strong work, Suzanne. And good to see you talking, Josh. See you two at twelve o'clock group."

I think I preferred the room stagnant. Our newfound chemistry was palpable, and Elliot knew it. As I watched him open and close the door, portions of the Lutheran Church liturgy began to play in my head—specifically, the moment in the service when the congregation asks forgiveness. Of course I wanted to work with Josh, but he'd opened the door into my most vulnerable self, a place I'd hardly visited on my own, let alone in the company of a handsome OxyContin addict. And he made me blush like a trollop!

"Suzanne? Are you okay?"

"Quid pro quo," I blurted out.

"Hunh?"

"I'll talk about my adoption story; you answer my questions for my assignment. Quid pro quo."

"Nice. I'm guessing I'm playing the role of Hannibal Lecter, Miss Starling?"

"Well, you are a doctor."

I'm pretty sure I was all-out flirting.

"And you a student," he nodded.

I began the questionnaire, taking notes as he recited his story. Born to an unwed mother, Josh was adopted by an Orthodox Jewish family at birth. When we shifted from his family history to his addiction history, he told me he first took opiates after getting his wisdom teeth pulled the summer after high school. For Josh, those two story lines became inextricably linked.

"I knew I was growing up in the wrong tribe, you know? I had this feeling of disconnect, of displacement. And when I took those pills for the first time, those out-of-sorts feelings disappeared. My world became soft and manageable for the first time."

He stopped and smiled, rubbing his hands together. "Your turn. So, have you met your birth mother?"

"Nope. Talked on the phone but never met her."

"Okay, so you found her?"

"Yes, with some help from the agency, but mostly on my own. But that was in 1999, eight years ago already. Your turn."

"Let me get this straight. You've found her. You've called her. But you haven't met her?"

I shook my head.

"Why not? You've got to meet her. Is it your adoptive parents? Are they not supportive?"

"Next question: When did your family and loved ones first become aware of your addiction?"

"Come on. Your story is more important than mine."

"No, it's not, Josh. I'm not the one in rehab. When did they know you were an addict?"

"Fine." He slouched back into his chair. "Med school. Mom called me out one night. I was pushing up against a wall in the kitchen, scratching my back like some wild animal. She ripped my glasses off and got in my face. I had pinpoint pupils and she just kept saying, 'Where are your pupils, Joshua? What did you do?' She got so tied up with the pupils."

"Guess she had to focus on something. Then what happened?"

"Nope, your turn. Why haven't you met your mom?"

I didn't want to tell him. I hadn't discussed it with anyone since Ariel.

"Hey," he said, touching my arm. "It's okay. You can tell me."

"It's not my adoptive parents. I haven't met my birth mom because two years ago, spring of 2005, on the day we planned to meet for the very first time, she didn't show up."

"What?"

"She was the one who suggested meeting in the first place. She said she'd be driving through my hometown, and she asked to come to my parents' house to meet me, meet them, and spend an hour or so together. Four o'clock on a Wednesday afternoon. So four o'clock came and went, and she never showed."

"But you know there had to be a reason, right?"

"I don't know anything."

"There had to be a reason. You need to call her."

"Has your addiction destroyed any meaningful relationships in your life or kept you from participating in meaningful relationships? If so, how?"

"Yes," he said in a flat tone. "I put my addiction before my family and my job. Now your turn."

"Wait!"

"I answered the question. Your turn." He planted his elbows on his knees like a coach. "Now listen to me. If there's one thing I can get out of this, it'll be knowing that you tried to contact your birth mom again."

I pushed back in my chair. This is exactly what Elliot had warned me about, the tables turning, the addict in the position of power. "I appreciate your concern, Josh, but it's not worth it."

"No. No," he said, his voice deepening, adamant. "It's painful, I know, but it's too important. People like us? We have to find our tribe. I don't know how old you are, but you're clearly not as fucked up as I am—at least not yet. But you have to find her. See her. Hear her voice. Then find out who your dad is. See him. Hear his voice. If you don't, you'll never know your own voice. You'll never know your whole self. Do you hear me? They are your tribe. You've got to call her again."

I sat in a stupor. I'd stepped through the looking glass with Josh, and in a matter of minutes, I'd have to walk back into my clinical rotation as if nothing had happened.

"Did you meet your parents?" I asked.

He nodded.

"And was it great? Was it what you'd hoped for?"

"It changed everything. It didn't fix my problems with drugs, but it's the one promise I've kept for myself, instead of trying to please everyone else. Finding my biological family—it's the nucleus, the core at the center of everything."

His words echoed my favorite Rumi poem:

The clear bead at the center changes everything.
There are no edges to my loving now.
I've heard it said there's a window that opens
from one mind to another,
but if there's no wall, there's no need
for fitting the window, or the latch.

Maybe Josh was right. Maybe finding my tribe would take the edge off my loving, take down some invisible, painful wall.

"Where'd you go again? Did you hear what I said?"

"Sorry, spaced out there," I sighed, checking my watch. "Almost done, and we only got through half of the dumb assignment."

Of course I heard him. But all my feelings about my biological family left me numb: my initial search, finding my mother, talking to her on the phone, making a date to meet, tossing and turning the night before, too nervous to eat the day of. And then she stood me up. Four o'clock turned into four thirty, then five, and still nothing. When I peeked out the windows of my parents' front door to see only Greenwood Cemetery across the street—no cars, no goddess mothers standing with anticipation at the end of the driveway—I closed a door inside myself. I pushed a big rock in front of the tomb, the place within me where I'd buried the relinquishment, the clear bead at my center that changes everything.

"Give me your paper," he said, pointing at the stack on my lap.

"What?"

"I'll fill out the rest of the questions if you'll do just one thing."

He tugged at the papers.

"Stop it! Tell me what this 'one thing' is before I agree to it."

"You have your mom's phone number, right?"

"Yes."

"Give me the papers."

I let go and put my head in my hands.

"You're stubborn." He smiled.

"You sound like my mother."

"Which one?"

"My *mother* mother—adoptive, you know."

"You give her a hard time?"

"We butt heads."

"My mom's a tough one, too," Josh said. "We can talk more about that tomorrow."

"Please," I said. "One mother at a time."

We laughed together, and a deep breath of common understanding filled the room.

"So, I will take the next couple of minutes and fill in answers to your assignment if you promise that within the next month, say, by Thanksgiving, you will call your mom. Deal?"

I caught myself staring too long into his eyes to indulge my nursing physical assessment skills: hazel irises, sclerae white and clear, pupils equal, reactive to light, 2–3 millimeters in diameter, now staring back into mine. I wanted to lay my head on his shoulder.

"Promise?" he asked again.

"Yes, Dr. Lecter."

"I'm not joking. Deal?" He reached out his hand.

"I know. I'm not either. I promise. I'll call."

"Come on, give me your hand."

I shook his hand and held on just a little too long—long enough to feel a question form in my mind, to hear my breath catch, to hope one of us had the sense to let go. Josh did, with a shy smile. He held the door as I gathered my things, and we walked down the hall to twelve o'clock group, fully expecting to see each other the next morning and take down a few more walls in our shared, secret mind.

But Josh was discharged that evening, his insurance provider no longer willing to reimburse inpatient treatment. Knowing I would never see him again, I was determined to keep my promise.

I called my birth mother on the Sunday after Thanksgiving during a flight delay at Denver International Airport, an ideal environment for me to fulfill my promise to Josh. I was a lone nursing student from Nebraska who had traveled from my home in New York to Colorado for a family holiday. But none of my circumstances mattered here. Airport travelers are equal in their anonymity, caught between departure and arrival, surrendered to the schedule and workings of the airlines and Mother Nature.

I gathered courage by cruising the mechanical walkways, invigorated by the possibility of travel to Seattle or Los Angeles or Mexico City. Airports are springboards, portals between destinations, and for me they had become a space where the invisible tension rod that suspends me between my two mothers relaxed, even disappeared.

Over the holiday I hadn't told my family about my psych rotation or Josh or my looming deadline. I'd kept the promise at bay, distracted by the joys of family traditions: Polish rummy, Cool Whip–based Jell-O "salads," cream of mushroom soup–Velveeta-vegetable casseroles topped with Durkee onions, and Grandma's annual testing of the sweet potatoes and predictable conclusion: "Needs a little salt."

No more thoughts of sweet potatoes with their toasty, marshmallow top. No more mechanical walkways. No more anything until I called my mother. If she answered, and if we spoke, nothing would change or everything would change. I opened my flip phone, scrolled to her number, and pressed the green call button.

One ring.

Two rings.

"Hello?" sounded a soft, woman's voice.

"Hello, may I please speak with Leah?"

A pause.

"This is Leah."

"Hi. This is Suzanne."

"Oh." Her voice broke. "Oh dear."

"Oh, no, if this is a bad time, I'm so sorry." I panicked, ready to hang up.

"No, no, stay on the line, please. I'm so glad you called."

# 6

## Gray

If I could have chosen the ideal time and place to meet my birth mother for the first time, it would not have been over the lunch hour at a gloomy sports bar. Inside, light filtered through streaky fingerprints on the windows and onto grease-stained carpet and torn vinyl seats. The smell of old kegs and stale ashtrays clung to the air, and Def Leppard's *Hysteria* album played overhead. But I would have met my mother at a sewage treatment plant if she had asked, or at a cemetery, or in clouds of methane at a feed lot.

As I drove west on the Lincoln Highway toward our lunch date, I wondered if I might be on the cusp of meeting the Holy Grail of my life, my mother herself a sacred relic of my mysterious past and, I hoped, the missing cornerstone that would click into my foundation and make me whole at the age of thirty-one. It was just after Christmas, the sky, the roads, the fields across Nebraska's central plains all the same, tired gray. When I first saw my mother getting out of her pickup, a look of fear flashed across her face as she braced against the wind. When I was born, she had just turned twenty-one so now would be over fifty. She had to work to stand and keep her balance, and I found in her short-clipped hair, ashen skin, and the smooth, dark half-moons beneath her eyes an echo of our cold, winter setting. I rushed to her and we hugged, the freezing wind from the south whistling around us. She felt cozy and soft in her parka, and I buried my head on her shoulder.

"I don't ever want to let you go," she whispered.

I squeezed tighter. I wanted to climb back inside of her and start all over.

She pulled me closer and said it again.

Though we embraced, though I'd traveled my whole life to find her and hear those very words, I discovered anew the truth we held between us: she had already let me go.

When I was in my early twenties, I was the live-in nanny for a toddler named Maia, the spirited only child of a couple who split their time between St. Paul, Minnesota, and the Upper West Side in Manhattan. When she reached her second birthday, the age when language development should blossom, Maia made only a couple of sounds, like "ha" and "ga." She used sign language to communicate not because she was hearing impaired but because her lips and tongue didn't have the strength and coordination to form words. She even signed in her sleep. Over the next year, her parents discovered a series of developmental delays, including apraxia of speech, a motor disorder. But Maia didn't need words to communicate. She read facial expressions, body language, and nonverbal cues. She knew what was said before it was spoken, at times demonstrating an intuition that bordered on savant.

While her parents were gone to dinner one evening, Maia played with blocks on the kitchen floor in their Manhattan apartment as I talked to my parents on the phone. My grandma on my dad's side had fallen and was hospitalized. Though the doctors thought she'd pull through, I despaired that I couldn't fly to Nebraska to see her. Maia watched me as she stacked her blocks, her wide, brown eyes full of concern.

I hung up and took a deep breath, ready to shift gears and be a happy caregiver. Maia patted her sticky fingers on my lap and tilted her head to the side with worry.

"Okay, kiddo, should we go for a walk?"

She patted my legs again, her signal for some lap time, so I hoisted her up and gave her a quick hug. "How about a visit to the park?"

She shook her head, reached her index finger out to my cheek, and traced it down my face like a tear.

"Oh, Maia." I pulled her to me. "How do you always know?"

She wrapped her arms around my neck and rubbed my shoulder in little toddler circles, then pulled back to reassess my emotional state. Unsatisfied, she squeezed me close again until I let myself go into a good, long cry.

I wish Maia could have come with me to that sports bar to meet my mom for the first time. Without someone there to ground us, Leah and I floated on the surface of ourselves, weaving in and out of pleasant conversation, yet disconnected. Halfway through nursing school, my senses were charged to assess people's health using the art of "thin slicing," as Malcom Gladwell calls it—employing intuition, instinct, and patterns, not just data, numbers, and words, to perceive someone or something. My mother looked like someone who didn't get enough sleep. I hadn't slept the night before either, but I had put myself together in a cheery, red sweater and clean pair of jeans. My mom's gray Nebraska football sweatshirt looked fresh and fluffed from the dryer and nearly hid the extra weight on her tall frame. She may have been tired, but she smelled like Downy fabric softener, and that comforted me.

Worried that I was staring too much, I focused on picking the raw onions out of my quesadilla and tuned in to the title track from Hysteria playing overhead. I'd never been able to decipher all the lyrics to Def Leppard songs, Joe Elliot's pronunciation being akin to Bob Dylan's, but on this day Elliot's words sang loud and clear.

Leah handed me a worn-out holiday gift bag. Inside she'd stuffed a pile of family photos, a hodgepodge of her other six children. Many of the pictures were dark or out of focus, the kind nobody would notice if they happened to go missing. After all, not one of my six siblings knew they had another sister, let alone that this person was sitting across from their mother at a sports bar.

"Out of touch," Joe Elliot's scratchy voice sang. "Out of reach, yeah."

I couldn't find myself in her face. For an instant when I first saw her in the parking lot—she craned her neck around to see if I was the person pulling up next to her in my parents' Buick, and I was—our eyes met. In that flash, the first time my own mother and I had ever looked at each other, I saw me in her. But the moment faded as quickly as it came. Not one of our features matched.

Out of touch. Out of reach. Exactly.

As I tried to muster the courage to ask her about my father, the William Blake poem that begins with "Little lamb who made thee" came to mind. I had sung the eerie John Tavener choral arrangement of the poem on Christmas Eve in New York just three days before. And because I knew I was about to meet my mother, I kept substituting the word *me* for *thee* during rehearsal. Little lamb who made *me*? Something about addressing my mother as "little lamb" resonated, for she'd sounded so soft and vulnerable on the phone when I'd called her from the Denver airport.

"I lost my son that day," she'd cried to me, her voice barely audible. On the day in 2005 when we were supposed to meet and she no-showed, my brother had died. When I asked her what had happened, I couldn't hear all her words—too many announcements over the loud speakers on my end, too many tears on hers. She said something about probation, something about a urine test and a stop sign and a wreck, and that he was dead at the hospital before she could say goodbye.

"I'm so sorry, Suzanne," she'd said. "I've lost two children in my life. Please help me get one of them back. Please give me a second chance."

Like the little lamb, whom Blake compares to Jesus in the second verse of his poem, my mother had sacrificed and suffered greatly. Now I'm not saying my birth mother is the Lord. But I recognize her sacrifice, and only she can answer my question.

Little lamb who made *me*?
Dost thou know who made *me*,
Gave me life and bid *me* feed
By the stream and o'er the mead?

I asked her about my father right as she took a bite of her club sandwich. Not one to talk with her mouth full, she acknowledged my question with a kind index finger and gave her sandwich a most thorough chewing as I waited in agony. This was more awkward than a blind date.

"I'm sorry to tell you this, but he's dead."

Not what I expected.

"And his name was Michael. Michael Erpelding."

Also not what I expected. My father was apparently a hobbit.

"Last year about this time, I believe. I read it in the paper."

Apparently troubling news does come in threes. First, I'll never meet him. Second, he sounds like some weird forest giant from Norse mythology. And last, had I been brave and tracked down Leah sooner, I could have met him. But I was stung from her no-show in 2005. I'd given up. And as I cowered in the corner of the rest of my life, I missed my dad.

She laughed at my reaction to his last name. And like any normal person who'd rather dwell on something comic than something tragic, I let the Erpelding name dance through my head for the rest of our lunch. For the record, Erpeldange (*Erpeldingen* is the German spelling) is a commune (a territorial division similar to a county in the United States) in Luxembourg that dates back to the thirteenth century. They even have a castle. In other words, yes, my people are from Middle-earth.

Leah wanted to know how I'd found her, so I started by telling her about Barbara, my adoption search social worker from Lutheran Family Services.

I waited two years for my name to reach the top of the search list, from the spring of my senior year of high school until the summer after my sophomore year of college. That's when I met Barbara, whom I actually like to call Babs, though never to her face. (Really, Babs is one of the best nicknames of all time. There's a knock-knock joke Chevy Chase delivers to Gilda Radner on *Saturday Night Live* that has the punch line "I don't know, Babs." That has become my chosen response to the many frustrating, ridiculous, and unanswerable questions that surface in life, and Babs has become a nickname for many of my closest friends, who, by virtue of our friendship, have joined in the Babs habit.)

So Babs found Leah through a series of letters that summer after my sophomore year of college. When they spoke by phone, Leah told Babs she'd kept me a secret, but she promised that she would tell her husband and children about me and then get back in touch with Babs by Christmas.

She never did.

By the time I graduated from college two years later, Babs had retired. When I called Babs's replacement in Omaha, she couldn't find my file and asked for more money to finance a continuation of the search.

"Wait, do you mean the search for my file? Or the search for my family?" I asked, truly unsure what I'd be paying for.

"The search, period," she replied with a hint of impatience. "Would you like to continue or not?"

*I don't know, Babs,* I wanted to say.

I sent another check, which did nothing to further my search. In fact, twenty years have passed since my file was first "misplaced," and it remains lost.

After leaving both grad school and an engagement at the age of twenty-three, I moved back in with my parents during the spring of 1999 and tracked down Babs through a call to information (this was before internet white pages). She was happy to help and "more than a little hacked off" at my birth mother.

"Had I known she wouldn't follow through on her word, I would never have told you about it! I could just throttle her." Babs had always made me laugh with her candor, but she admitted she'd become a touch more "vindictive" in her retirement.

Here's what she remembered from my story: My birth mother had a son before me from a different father. She had kept the child and given him an uncommon name. Babs suggested I visit Kearney, the last town she associated with my birth mother, and start by searching in old newspapers for my brother's name. Thus I made my first investigative trip to Kearney and used my brother's first name, along with Leah's, to guide me through five hours of newspaper microfiche searching at the Kearney Public Library.

Nothing.

On to Kearney High School and a yearbook search.

Nothing.

If it hadn't been for a guidance counselor in coach pants and a matching shirt—with Jim embroidered over the left breast and a whistle around his neck—strolling into the conference room where I sat buried in yearbooks, I would have given up. If Jim hadn't asked my story, all the while bouncing the eraser of his mechanical pencil in fast, staccato rhythm on the table (Jim coached football and conducted conversation with the urgency of a fourth-quarter time-out), I would have left Kearney High School and laid my search to rest, maybe forever.

Jim and I stacked up the yearbooks and walked down to the lobby outside of his office to meet Linda, his secretary, "a gal who knows everyone in Buffalo County." When Jim asked her if she ever knew a kid with my big brother's name, Linda nodded, tilting her head to the right as she gathered her thoughts.

"You know, there was that family that lived behind us on Twenty-Eighth whose oldest son had that name. Lovely neighbors. What was that gal's first name . . . was it Leah? Yes, Leah, that's right. Last saw her at the grocery store before they moved up to Humbleton. Why do you ask?"

I stared at her, my mouth agape.

Jim took us both by the elbows and steered us into his office. When I told Linda my story, she burst into tears, which made me wonder why I wasn't crying. Jim just kept scribbling notes on scratch paper as we talked—details about the family, the little town up north they'd moved to, the younger brother who'd played for the basketball team in the state championship just weeks before. In less than two minutes, Jim, Linda, and I had morphed from three strangers into the Three Musketeers, explorers who'd unearthed a long-kept secret. But their excitement quickly shifted to parental concern. They made me promise to take my time with the new information, to consider how this could affect people on both sides of the secret, and to maybe just write a letter and not expect too much in return. (Nebraska culture forbids us from getting our hopes up.)

I hugged them goodbye, stuffed the mess of scratch paper into my bag, and sped twenty miles north to see my mother's house—my other family's house! The gravel roads kicked rocks up under the car as I whipped around to take my first pass through the little town of less than four hundred people. Their house sat on a corner lot just past the football field—blue, two stories, with black, cast iron porch columns around the front and a couple of dogs in the back.

On my third lap, I remembered I was in rural Nebraska and that a Buick Regal from Seward County would draw attention if I stayed any longer, so I left. I drove east on Highway 2 past Ravenna toward Grand Island, my birthplace, and realized I'd traveled that route before as a child, headed from a family funeral in Kearney (yes, Great Aunt Hulda of the embarrassing photograph taken by my grandpa Ohlmann) to the burial in Ravenna. I'd driven past my birth mother's town and not even known it.

From the moment I left Kearney High School, I felt like Paul Revere, galloping my horse over hill and dale, the biggest news of my life on the tip of my tongue. I squeezed the steering wheel and screamed "I found my mom!" over and over, my entire body an instrument vibrating with the same, thrilling message.

I stopped for gas in Grand Island before driving the final eighty miles to Seward and bought a celebratory soft-serve cone at the truck stop. I dialed up Mom in Seward from a pay phone, bursting with my news. After a long pause, she asked me if I would be home on time for supper.

"Mom, I'm in Grand Island. It's five o'clock. I won't be home for an hour."

She exhaled.

"Mom?"

She'd been so supportive of my quest, but when the act of seeking transformed into the act of finding a real person who lived in a real place, I think Mom felt threatened.

"I told you to be home by five thirty."

I said goodbye and chucked my cone into the trash with a *thwump*.

Back at the sports bar, Leah and I rose to leave. As I futzed around with my zipper, she tossed me a curveball.

"Should we go and meet your grandma?"

"What?" I asked.

"She'll be glad to see you. It's not far. Just follow me—we'll get you home on time for supper."

"But does she know I'm coming?"

She climbed into her pickup. I wasn't sure how old her mother was, but as I followed Leah through the snowy streets, I hoped my new grandma would have a strong heart. I wasn't ready to practice CPR that day.

The drive from Kearney to Seward takes two hours, and Mom had agreed to push supper back to six o'clock, giving me ample time to make it home after lunch. But then Leah took me to meet my grandma, Dolores, the only family member who had held me when I was born. When we arrived at her place, Leah went to the door while I hid in the porch shadows.

"Mom," she said. "I have a surprise for you."

"Oh hell, Leah, what is it now?" Dolores said, still out of my line of sight.

Grandma didn't seem to like surprises.

"Suzanne is here," Leah whispered.

"Wait, now what's that, Leah?"

"You heard me, Mom. Suzanne."

Dolores let out a brief, high-pitched sob, then stepped over the threshold to see me.

"Where did all that dark hair go?" she cried and held out her arms.

After a good, long hug, she stepped back to give me the once-over with wide blue eyes set behind red-rimmed, Sally Jesse Raphael glasses. Then she smacked Leah on the arm. "You bring her home and can't give your mother five minutes' notice to comb her hair? For heaven's sakes, Leah, I look like I just got off my broom."

I thought she looked sharp in her navy pants, navy-and-white Scandinavian-style sweater, and curled, white hair. She was sassy and self-deprecating, and she couldn't be bothered with pretense. My newfound grandma reminded me of the person I hoped to be in the world.

The three of us visited in Dolores's living room, my mother and I on the couch, Dolores in her recliner, all of us laughing together at her over-the-top Christmas decor, the foundation of which was a Christmas forest floor made of green-tinted Saran wrap dotted with puffs of fake snow from the local craft store.

"We're high class in this family, Suzanne." Dolores gestured to the grove of fake Christmas trees adorning her TV console. "Not a penny spared."

When Dolores caught wind of my mother's strict mealtimes, she hugged me close and shooed me out the door. Neither she nor Leah was big on long goodbyes. I sped home in the Buick, pushing the seventy-five-miles-per-hour speed limit on I-80, sure I would be late for dinner. Thirty-one years old and a nursing student at an Ivy League school, and I might as well have been a teenager about to miss curfew.

Guilt gave way to thoughts of the death of my father, Michael Erpelding, and the laughs I'd conjured from his Tolkien name faded with the daylight behind me. I had just met my biological mother, had just started climbing back into the story of my birth, and WHOOSH! *Death.* No more fantasies or standing on my tiptoes to slice Sam Shepard a piece of cake. Michael was my dad, and Michael was dead.

Leah told me at lunch that she had kept up with him in the newspaper over the years. She had read that he'd gotten married, that they had had a baby girl, that the baby girl had died before her first birthday.

"Seems like you loved him," I said.

"Yeah," she said as she looked past me. "I did."

I felt relieved.

"He was a huge part of my life, but I'm not sure he even would have remembered me. I was pretty good at picking the bad ones. Hope you've had better luck."

*Whoops*, I thought, and I worked to keep the focus on her. Now was not the time to shift into gal-pal-man-story mode.

"I feel really bad about that," she said.

"About what? That you loved him?"

"No, no. That he died thinking he'd lost his only daughter."

"He didn't know?"

"No." She shook her head. "I should have told him about you."

I wish I had asked Leah more questions. I wish I had listened better. I wish I had been more loving, more demonstrative, more connected to myself and able to connect with her. I wish I had looked at Leah with Maia's clear eyes and heart, and that Leah had looked at me in the same way. Even numb, we fumbled our way toward the truth. Our semifrozen state was the only thing keeping us sitting there at the table and not splayed across that greasy carpet. I thought being numb meant a person wasn't feeling enough. But as Leah and I sat across from each other that late December having lunch as mother and daughter for the first time, each of us was tired from a lifetime of feeling too much.

I can see myself blazing east on the interstate, a heavy sadness filling the car as I try to stay awake and make it back to Seward on time. I can see Leah and Dolores side by side on Dolores's couch, retelling stories of the day they got their baby back. I can see my mother in her kitchen, checking the clock. 6:01 p.m. Her daughter is late. She looks out the window, no cars on North Second Street, no headlights in the distance, just the cemetery and a streetlight blinking on. Mom's never been late in her life.

I didn't consider Mom's nerves when I walked through the kitchen door and past her glare at 6:10 p.m., making a beeline to the office to search for Michael Erpelding's obituary on the internet. I didn't consider that her need to control my timeframe might have been born out of anxiety or that all three of us, daughter, mother, and mother, might have met with an uncomfortable vulnerability that day. I couldn't think about my mom's feelings. I couldn't really think at all.

I sat at the computer and read my father's obituary as Mom called me for supper. "Coming!" I shouted back while scanning the lines, wishing I could skip dinner and crawl into bed.

CHANDLER, Ariz. - Michael E. Erpelding, 51, of Chandler, formerly of Kearney, Neb., died Saturday, Dec. 23, 2006, in Chandler.

Memorial services will be at 2 p.m. Monday at Horner-Lieske-Horner Mortuary in Kearney with the Rev. Dean Pofahl officiating. Burial will be at Kearney Cemetery.

There will be no visitation.

He was born Dec. 14, 1955, in Kearney to Donald and Donna (Clark) Erpelding.

In July 1983, he married Karen Hoffmeier.

He grew up and attended school in Kearney.

He worked for Kearney Concrete then moved to Arizona in 1986 where he had lived since.

He enjoyed hunting, camping and woodworking and collected many things. He loved being with his family and friends and was always there in times of need. He will be greatly missed by everyone in his life he touched.

He was preceded in death by his infant daughter, Stacey, and his parents.

Memorials are suggested to the family.

"Suzy," Dad said as he came into the office. "Better come and eat." He put his hand on my shoulder and looked down his bifocals at the screen. "This is your father, is it?"

He whispered the words of the obituary aloud as he read and took a tissue from his front pocket. "So sad," he said. "He'll never know the miracle he left behind."

I closed the browser and leaned into Dad's arm.

"For the last time, dinner . . . is . . . served!" Mom yelled down the hall, her hands cupped around her mouth like a teacher on a playground.

"Coming, Mama. Coming."

# 7

## Shadow Dad

As a member of the St. Olaf Choir, I spent a lot of time on concert stages in a purple velvet robe, nude hose, and a pair of black, smelly flats—smelly because all the women's shoes traveled in the same trunk from tour venue to tour venue, to limit the risk of someone violating the strict dress code during performance. The choir maintained a uniform appearance because, though made up of seventy-five members, it functioned as one, vibrant organism. We held hands, we sang from memory, and we swayed as we sang. Not wild movement—we were young Lutherans following in the footsteps of a century-long tradition—but if you attended a performance, you couldn't help but notice the way the music moved in subtle waves through the group.

I made it into choir my junior and senior years at St. Olaf and found it a welcome community in which to pursue my study and development as a musician. During my senior year, Dr. Armstrong, the conductor, appointed me soprano section leader as well as one of three student conductors of the group, both high honors. But I'd also stumbled into my first bout of clinical depression, and by early December, when we taped the PBS broadcast of our 1997 Christmas Festival, I was barely making it to rehearsals and classes, surviving on a twenty-milligram daily dose of Paxil, an antidepressant.

Two months later, in early February, we embarked on our Southwest tour, and our first stop was a weekend of concerts in and around

Phoenix. The area held no significance for me at the time, but I now know that my birth father lived the final years of his life in Chandler, a Phoenix suburb, and would have been living there at the time of the tour. I wish he could have come to the show, but by my senior year, I'd all but given up on finding anyone in my biological family. More than two years had passed since my last conversation with the social worker, Babs, at Lutheran Family Services. Her final report, written just before my sophomore year at St. Olaf, said that my birth mom was supposed to reveal my secret existence to her family and that I'd be welcomed at Christmas with open arms. Her silence made it clear she hadn't.

We sang a Sunday afternoon concert at Symphony Hall in downtown Phoenix. My very old and generous Uncle Don and Aunt Ruth, snowbirds from Iowa, came to the performance with their friends from church, Blanche and Paul. Afterward, they drove me east for dinner in Fountain Hills, their retirement community. I sat in the back of Don's pearly white Cadillac sedan and became Blanche's captive audience while Paul slept and Aunt Ruth daydreamed. Uncle Don never could hear so well.

"Suzy," Blanche beamed, "I want you to look straight ahead at those red rock mountains."

I followed her gaze.

"Do you see anything?" she asked.

The sun had begun its descent behind us, the rock formations ahead blazing a bright burnt sienna in the late afternoon light. I wasn't sure what I was looking for.

"They say that when the sun hits those mountains just right, you can see the face of Jesus the Christ." Blanche smiled with such fervor that I could hear saliva crackling behind her teeth.

I sat with my mouth open.

"Isn't that just wonderful?"

I love Aunt Ruth and Uncle Don, and I have to giggle at anyone who ups the ante of a story by inserting "the" between "Jesus" and "Christ." However, giggling makes me feel like a bad Lutheran, because we all know that Christ was not his actual last name, and thus "the Christ" is correct. But it's kind of like saying "the cancer." It just sounds funny, and when Blanche said it, I found myself looking for an eject button in the back of Don's Cadillac.

Why couldn't Mike Erpelding have come to hear me sing in Phoenix and saved me from Blanche's messianic vision? My favorite piece from the concert was by Mendelssohn, "For God Commanded Angels to Watch Over You," and I have to wonder if those angels couldn't have done something more to intervene and give Mike and me the chance to meet, take a walk, snap some photos, feel each other's presence in that dry, desert air; or even just sneak out early one morning for a quick breakfast at Denny's. He'd order some godawful Grand Slam number with piles of bacon and hash browns, and I'd get the oatmeal or raisin bran, something ridden with fiber to try to keep my bowels moving as I sat in awe, with a slight touch of panic, watching my dad eat and drink and laugh and look back at me.

I have this fantasy that if I could have met him that weekend, somehow the trajectory of both of our lives would have been altered for the better. All the darkness that had begun to consume me that fall, but for my weekly therapy sessions and the Paxil, the dread that had seeped into my life in such an insidious manner—affecting my appetite, sleep, concentration, and moods, my menstrual cycle, and even my will—surely it had come from an old, inherited sadness that I would have to wait twenty years to comprehend.

And what about Mike? When I finally found the Erpeldings—first through letters, then emails, then phone calls and repeated, welcoming visits—they didn't want to state the truth about Mike in plain English. But I don't share their name. I carry the weight of loss but am freed by never having known him. So I can say that my father died alone just after his fifty-first birthday. He was found in the bedroom of his trailer at the Sunshine Valley Mobile Home Park on South Arizona Avenue in Chandler, his death caused by alcoholism and hepatitis C cirrhosis of the liver, the result of a lifelong addiction to Old Milwaukee and all that heroin in the 1970s.

Surely I could have helped him. We were the same person, just in different incarnations. At least that's what I wanted to believe as I uncovered the layers surrounding his life and death. He wasn't my soulmate but the author of my existence, creator of my core, and, even dead, fantastical sustainer of my belief that what I had lost in him had meant something. He'd even provided an excuse for my accident-prone nature. An entire page of his fiftieth birthday book was devoted to his calamities, including:

- cut off his thumb with a saw
- put a barrel through the rear window of his Vega
- burned Vega to a crisp in front of girlfriend's house
- started Kearney Livestock on fire
- broke his back twice

Or as noted in this text conversation between Uncle Greg and me:

ME: Hi, Uncle Greg! Random question: Do you remember the car Mike was driving around 1975? I'm trying to picture him the summer he and my mom were together and I was conceived.

UNCLE GREG: How you doing, girl? Mike had so many cars in that time of his life. It could have been a '57 Chevy, a '66 Impala. A '72 Vega wagon is what I think it was. He had many cars and wrecked every one of them.

But back in Arizona, in February of my senior year, I was twenty-one and Mike forty-two. Had I been more tenacious or even demanding with Lutheran Family Services, just maybe they could have gotten his name from Leah in that single phone call she had with Babs. I could have kept his name a secret. I could have chased away my depression just knowing that my father was in Phoenix and that on the day of our downtown concert, I'd make my escape to meet him, with or without the help of angels.

St. Olaf Choir has a way of caring for its own. If a member should grow faint during a performance, she signals her peril to the singers on either side of her with a series of quick hand squeezes. The other two move in a stealth manner to step in front and around her so she can sit down on the risers and hang her head between her knees—all of this without a moment's rest from the music.

I could have "fainted," gone down on the risers, the choir surrounding me in a wall of velvet, and slipped under the stage through the trap door. In seconds I could have exited onto Third Street in downtown Phoenix, hailed a cab, and been on my way to Chandler. I would have laughed the whole way at my costume for our first father-daughter meeting.

I was so pale and pure then, still a virgin, not that keen on booze, and a music major worried most about singing in tune and remembering the dates of Beethoven's early, middle, and late periods for Music History exams. I had my senior recital to plan, graduate school auditions to prepare for, and a very loving boyfriend who'd somehow stuck with me through the crying spells and incessant napping that had overcome me.

I had no business meeting Mike Erpelding that day in Phoenix, but what if I had? What if I'd walked up to trailer number 275, knocked on the screen door, and found a way to explain both the reason I was there and the fact that I was dressed in a purple velvet robe with nothing underneath but Hanes Her Way underpants and my stinky shoes?

Maybe Mike could have lived a little longer.

Maybe I could have lived a little lighter.

My Erpelding family never lied to me about Mike, but they were cautious in their portrayal of their beloved brother, almost curating his image in the wake of his early death. Though Mike lived and died under the shadow of addiction, I would learn over the years that he was a loving, cherished, charismatic, present force in the lives of his family and friends. My first step toward finding him, before I revealed the surprise of my existence to his family, was to visit his grave. Before I gathered the courage to write to them, I had to see for myself that this long-imagined man was already gone.

Kearney Cemetery sits on the north side of town, a clean, vast space set across a series of low-cresting hills. Six months after my first meeting with Leah, I'd driven to Kearney for another lunch with her, this time at an Italian place in a different strip mall, with better food, better lighting, and summer sunshine to brighten the atmosphere. Once again I'd borrowed my parents' Buick and had to be home on time for supper. Though we conversed throughout the meal, mostly small talk about Leah's other children, I don't remember anything except the following exchange, which struck me like a two by four to the head:

"You said that my birth father used to have wild parties. What kind of 'wild' do you mean?" I asked her.

"Everything. Needles," she said, not once looking up from her pasta bowl. "Can you please pass the parmesan cheese?"

With that little nugget playing on a loop in my mind, I pulled through the graveyard entry gates. My dad had warned me that morning that Kearney Cemetery was large and that it would be "nearly impossible to find anyone without directions." He would know because we Ohlmanns had buried a good number of family members there over the years. Although many relatives had been buried out at the country church the family founded when they first settled the land, others, like Grandpa O's twin brother Erwin, were laid to rest at Kearney Cemetery.

Minding Dad's advice, when I got to the cemetery I marched over to the computer directory and promptly discovered it was broken. With little time and even less direction, I started at the western edge of the grounds and passed Baby Hill, the plots saved for the burials of infants and children. After an endless ten minutes of serpentine cruising through lane after lane, I shifted into panic mode, my hands clammy as I scanned another row of unfamiliar families.

"Please, Daddy, help me find you!" I pounded my hands on the steering wheel.

I don't know where "Daddy" came from. Glenn Ohlmann was my dad, not this strange man with an even stranger name who never even knew I existed. Who was I hoping to find in that green expanse of dead people?

Knowing I had just minutes before I needed to leave Kearney and drive home to supper, I turned down a new row and eased past each stone, the first one black, then a gray one, then another and another. A white stone appeared with the name ERPELDING engraved across the front, and I jammed on the brakes. I parked the Buick and walked slow steps to the gravestone. Grass clippings from the morning's mow were strewn across its ledge, and faded silk flowers drooped from a metal vase on the side. On the back, a tarnished brass marker affixed to the lower left-hand corner of the stone bore Mike's name. I fell to my knees and ran my fingers over his birth and death dates: December 14, 1955–December 23, 2006. This stranger who created me came and went at Christmas time, a thought that made me heave with sadness. I tried to buff the marker with a corner of my shirt, then crawled around the stone to sweep off the grass. Satisfied I'd given at least the intention of cleaning, I grabbed my camera and took a photo, puzzling over why he had been buried with his parents. This would be my first taste of Mike's poverty.

A gust of wind blew up from the south. If I wanted to get home by supper, I needed to leave at that very moment, but time had begun to soften. White clouds streamed over from west to east, shape-shifting, the world quiet but for a meadowlark in a nearby cottonwood. A gentle, twisting cyclone stirred around me and swept me up into that fantastical space where Mike and I could meet and breathe the same air. We could have found ourselves in each other: toothy grins, sloping noses, dimpled cheeks, broad shoulders, long legs, ready laughs, crooked fingers, and the familiar, echoing sadness deeply sewn into our cells, mine soothed with therapy and antidepressants, his with beer. But we never would, and so the wind set me down on the warm grass. I missed supper, cradling myself on the bed of Mike's grave, his absence from my life suddenly real and heavy.

# 8

## *Doppelgänger*

Three years after Mike died—after I'd visited his grave, moved to San Antonio, and put in a good year of work as a full-time, intensive care nurse—I cared for a patient named Leonard who was the spitting image of Jesus the Christ.

It was the week of Christmas when Leonard became my patient, though he had been hospitalized since before Thanksgiving. He was fifty years old and smelled like sweat, sour breath, and incontinent bowels. Before I'd been assigned to Leonard's care, every one of his major organ systems had failed—even his skin. His entire body was covered in large, fluid-filled welts called *bullae*. He was dependent on a mechanical ventilator because of respiratory failure and was connected to the machine by a tracheostomy tube surgically inserted into his throat. His blood pressure and heart were sustained by three different intravenous medications, and his failed kidneys were replaced with hemodialysis, the blood from his body washed by an intricate filtering mechanism the size of a vending machine. He had tubes in every orifice, nostrils to anus. Alone and with his nearest family a thousand miles away in Georgia, Leonard's comatose state left him completely vulnerable to the whims of his medical team. He was incapable of closing his eyes, his stare casting an eerie spell over the room until we decided to start taping his eyelids shut for two-hour intervals. Nurses clucked their tongues upon hearing his story, shaking their heads at his plight in a combination of disbelief and indignation, whispering, "He should have known better" or, my favorite, "People like that are the reason I'm not an organ donor."

Leonard was an alcoholic and had hepatitis C, most likely from IV drug use, but it's possible he wasn't aware of his diagnosis. When he decided to party with his fellow migrant construction workers at a seafood joint north of San Antonio, he should have had the fish and chips. But he ordered a plate of raw oysters, fresh from the Gulf of Mexico. Maybe one of Leonard's physicians had warned him about raw oysters and hepatitis C. Maybe Leonard knew that because he had hep C, he shouldn't drink alcohol; that his immune system was weakened by his ailing liver; that raw or undercooked seafood from the warm waters of the Gulf sometimes carries a monster bacteria called *Vibrio vulnificus*; that a person with hep C who contracts *Vibrio vulnificus* faces a 50–85 percent mortality rate from infection and septic shock. Maybe Leonard knew, but I doubt it. I can't say that he should have known better.

If Mike had known better and skipped the needles and beer, he might have lived long enough to meet me. Then again, addiction is like any disease; it lives outside the bounds of logic. If I wanted to know Mike, I needed to communicate with his family. A year before I met Leonard, I drummed up the courage to write to the Erpeldings. I sent identical letters and a photograph to my father's two siblings, Aunt Christine and Uncle Greg. I'd found their names in his obituary and located their address using a free white pages website. They both replied within a week with a warm welcome, setting my relationship with the Erpeldings in stark contrast to my decade-long struggle to reconnect with my birth mother.

I also heard from my cousin Chelsey, Greg's daughter, who I'd learn was Mike's biggest fan.

Dear Suzanne,

I would love to tell you more about Mike. He was such a great guy. When he died, all I could tell people is that he had a heart of gold. He was such a family guy. He would have loved to know you. He cared so much about his family. I really wish you would have known him.

Take care, Chelsey

Chelsey very quickly became an integral part of my life. After an exchange of emails, we made plans to meet in Nebraska the following Christmas. We had sushi in Lincoln (hey, coastal people snickering at the very idea—they fly it in, and it tastes delicious) for our first date. Months later, when I was home, we met and made paint-your-own-pottery bowls together. At dinner that night, she caught me bantering with the waiter about which of two entrées I should order—large menus give me anxiety—and when he walked away, she said, "You reminded me of Mike just then. He could make anybody laugh, usually by making fun of himself. I miss him. I'm glad I know you."

It's hard not to reach across the booth and kiss a person when she says something like that, especially when you've waited your entire life to hear someone say that you remind them of a fellow family member. My parents, along with Grandma and Grandpa A, once told me that I reminded them of Great-Grandpa Ahrens, but they were not giving me much of a compliment. Great-Grandpa was an alcoholic, and when he came home drunk, both his wife and Grandma A would lecture him on the public humiliation he caused the family. When they were finished, he would look them in the eye and say, without an ounce of sarcasm, "Thank you."

Apparently I said this same kind of thank-you on several occasions after receiving a scolding from my mother. I did so while visiting Grandma and Grandpa A once and nearly brought the house down. I will say that I distinctly remember a twinkle in Grandpa's eye while they explained the story, similar to Chelsey's face beaming at me from across that booth.

After the initial exchange of letters and emails, Uncle Greg wanted to talk on the phone. When I called, he told me that Mike was his big brother and best friend; that Mike never missed a birthday; that he loved to work with his hands and had a bit of a mail-order problem.

"He sure did love his knick-knacks," he said.

I asked him, "How did Mike die?"

"Mike liked to drink Old Milwaukee."

I laughed. "Really? Old Mill?" I asked.

"Yeah, I never liked that stuff—got a real twang to the taste—but Mike drank it for breakfast."

I laughed again. "Breakfast?" I asked.

"Yeah. Let's see, there was the beer, and Mike partied pretty hard in the seventies, you know how it was: live hard, die young," he said.

"Yeah," I lied, thinking of my parents, who spent the seventies singing in the St. John Lutheran Church choir, socializing at potlucks in the church basement, and practicing recorder for their weekly recorder group. We have photos documenting Dad playing a polished, wooden, tenor recorder, a bowl of black hair on his head, my mom in a hand-sewn denim suit with red pin stripes, blonde highlights in her hair, and cocktail glasses of soda pop within reach of each of them.

Uncle Greg continued. "We're pretty sure Mike had hepatitis from all that partying, so that didn't help with the beer."

"Hepatitis? Which hepatitis?" I asked.

"Well," he said, "we're thinking it was probably hep C that got Mike in the end. Hep C and beer."

So there it is. I knew that my biological father had died of hep C and beer when I cared for Leonard. I even had the information when I took the job in that particular liver/kidney transplant hospital. But it lived in my subconscious mind and never informed my decision making—not in my choice to leave New York and move to San Antonio, not in my job search, not even during the interview with the nurse manager. When she asked why I'd decided to pursue intensive care, I told my future boss that I wanted to work in a setting that would expose me to the widest variety of illness and teach me the most about nursing in the shortest amount of time.

"You'll be right at home here," she chirped, her heels clicking across the floor when we toured the hospital during my interview. As we passed the rooms, she barked out the illness of each of the twenty patients on the unit. "This guy's a postop triple A with blood pressure issues, and we're about to put him on a nitro drip. And here we have a fresh kidney transplant. Just look at the sparkling urine in that Foley bag. Bed four is a total septic train wreck. Bed five is an ESLD/hep C/cirrhosis awaiting transplant and headed down the drain with a new viral infection. And bed six? Oh yes, overdose, on a vent, on a Narcan drip; he came in through the ER last night. You get the picture? Sound like what you're looking for?"

Though overwhelmed by the multiple diagnoses, all I could see was a green light. This was my job. This was my next adventure.

"Just one quick question," I said. "What's ESLD?"

"End-stage liver disease. You'll become an expert on it if you join our team. And don't worry about any of the terms or disease processes. You went to a good school. You'll pick it up as you go."

I moved to San Antonio and started the job just after Christmas, eager to master a new set of skills. I worked overtime and followed written orders and hospital protocols. I helped my fellow nurses clean and turn their patients, studied up on the advanced cardiac life support protocols to get my certification, jumped into codes (cardiac and respiratory arrests), cracked ribs with chest compressions, pushed meds, called out times, and donned gowns, gloves, and splash masks when things got messy. In a matter of months, I'd transformed from a freelance musician/nursing student in New York to a full-time ICU nurse in San Antonio.

Though I had begun to learn about Mike and hep C, I hadn't found a way to comprehend his life or how it related to mine. In this new realm of intensive care nursing, many hepatitis C patients had contracted the disease from needles in the 1970s and now needed a liver transplant. Many were men in their early fifties with long hair, mustaches and beards, tattoos, and missing teeth—not a group you often find in

Lutheran churches or St. Olaf Choir concerts. I grew to love them as my patients and soon learned that these men were part of a tribe I would come to call my own.

By the time I met Leonard during the holiday season, a year had passed since I'd first connected with the Erpeldings. I'd been working the night shift for most of that year, fully succumbing to vampire hours, awake for shorter and shorter amounts of daylight as fall turned to winter.

I'd begun to disconnect with conventional life, partly due to my sleep schedule and partly due to the trauma I tended to throughout each twelve-hour shift. We had stretches where we lost a patient almost every night, most often those with ESLD who bled to death or whose lungs filled with fluid or whose depressed immune systems fell prey to nasty bacteria. My work had consumed my life. I did little other than laundry, watch replays of Spurs games, and sleep.

On my first night with Leonard, "Feliz Navidad" piped over the hospital speakers while a janitor mopped the hallway outside Leonard's room, humming along. Two nurses stood over Leonard's bed to change the linens, and Leonard lay on his side facing out, his crystal blue eyes staring past me. He was on contact isolation for a drug-resistant bacterial infection, which required any personnel entering his room to don protective gear. I'd be spending the next four nights in a gauzy yellow gown and blue medical gloves, so I was content to chat from my post outside the room amidst the flurry of soiled linens and sanitary wipes.

"And he has so much gas." Trent, Leonard's day nurse, scrunched up his nose. "I'll show you."

"Please, no, I believe you," I begged from the doorway.

Trent began gently kneading Leonard's abdomen like a bowl of dough, a chorus of flatulence blasting from his backside like the bellows of a blacksmith. "Well, it can't be comfortable for him," Trent shouted over the gales of wind wafting into the hall, "all bloated and full of all that gas and poop."

"You have a point." I plugged my nose. "Will you stop the Christmas Fart Fest and give me your report?"

I looked back at Leonard's face, my eyes locked with his empty gaze. I couldn't admit to anyone that I thought Leonard looked like Jesus and that music from *Messiah* rushed into my head whenever I saw him. *He was despised.* I heard the alto sing, low and mournful with the sighing string accompaniment. *Despised and rejected.* Brown hair, mustache, beard, piercing blue eyes; this is the Jesus I grew up with in Nebraska. Leonard's cheeks were less rosy, covered with skin lesions and overgrown facial hair, and jaundiced from the liver failure. But even unkempt and yellow, Leonard was a Jesus doppelgänger.

I tried to compliment him when I spoke to his mother on her nightly 8:30 p.m. phone calls.

"How's my sonny?" she'd ask in a thin, scratchy voice.

"He has such beautiful blue eyes," I'd say, after listing his maladies and overall poor prognosis.

"Oh, thank you, honey. He sure does. But how can you see them if he's sleeping all the time? I thought he was asleep?"

This is the danger of looking for a silver lining in the realm of intensive care or deciding your patients look like the Lord. Every connection you make between a patient and something or someone familiar to you, even something ridiculous like a celebrity or a religious figure, makes you more connected to them as a person. An intimacy is born, and thus the sense of loss is greater when they die.

"He's in a special kind of sleep called a coma, ma'am, and he can't close his eyes. So we see them a lot, and they are beautiful."

"Oh." She paused, then continued in a softer voice. "I see. Well, you take good care of my boy."

She ended all of our conversations with those words. I imagined her sitting at a small, drop-leaf table in a kitchen with peeling, flowery wallpaper. She resembled the woman in *American Gothic*, but she was sweeter and smaller in her apron and wire-rimmed glasses, her white hair tied back in a bun. She was frail and tired and helpless, thousands of miles away from her dying son, a son who should have known better.

Leonard's stare unnerved even the most veteran of nurses, and we took turns on Leonard duty due to the rigors of his care and the psychological toll of his grim state. I coped by singing to him. No matter what task or medication brought me into his room, I sang to him from a lifetime catalog of Christmas music. Leonard lay still in the bed, unresponsive to verbal, physical, and even painful stimuli, and I sang. The music kept the two of us company. I sang in soft tones, wanting to fill his room with sounds other than the beeps of the IV pumps, the heaves and sighs of the ventilator, and the alarms of his cardiac monitor.

My nursing colleagues laughed at me if they walked past and heard my quiet Christmas concert in Leonard's corner room. They didn't know that I'd grown up in the Ohlmann family, a family with its own four-part chorus. Dad sang tenor, Mom alto, Jeff bass baritone (after the age of fifteen), and I soprano. Lutherans are prone to harmonizing when they sing. Church organists accompany hymns through the first verse or two, then drop out to let the congregation morph into a choir, which we do nimbly, almost instinctively. Singing is encouraged, even expected, and ever since Bach's time, the emphasis has been on choral music and congregational singing, not on solos. (As a Lutheran, you wouldn't want to draw too much attention to your voice, even if it were beautiful.) Once I branched out as a soprano soloist in college, my mom would often remind me, "Don't be a diva, Suzanne."

When I was little, both Mom and Dad sang in the church choir, with Dad the occasional cantor/soloist. Each year during Holy Week, he chanted a psalm at the end of the Maundy Thursday service. After communion the head usher turned down the lights in the nave as the ministers began stripping the altar. In the darkened church, Dad's raw, tenor voice pierced the silence with the words of Psalm 22.

My God, my God, why have you abandoned me?
Why are you so far from helping me, from the words of my
    groaning?
O my God, I cry out by day, but you do not answer; and by night,
    but find no rest.
My God, my God, why have you abandoned me?

I never knew who to watch, my dad in the balcony behind me or
the pastors at the front of the church, dismantling the altar in somber,
mournful gestures. But were they mournful? Or was it my dad and his
pleading music that set the tone?

But I am a worm, and not human; scorned by others and despised
    by the people.
All who see me mock me; they make mouths at me, they shake
    their heads.
My God, my God, why have you abandoned me?

Polite churchgoers don't turn around to see who's singing in the
balcony; an expression of such obvious curiosity would be considered
untoward. But he was my dad, so I craned my neck to see him in the
soft glow of his music stand light, eyebrows furrowed, shoulders rising
with a deep breath before each phrase.

On you I was cast from my birth, and since my mother bore me
you have been my God.
Do not be far from me, for trouble is near and there is no one to help.
My God, my God, why have you abandoned me?

Dad got busy with work at the library and eventually quit the choir.
Once I grew up and left home for college at St. Olaf, I took the mantle
from Dad and started singing solos from the balcony during holidays
and summers at home. But I never sang Psalm 22—not on any Sunday
nor Maundy Thursday. The solo is better sung by a man to evoke the voice
of Jesus as he died, the antiphon some of his last words from the cross.

I am poured out like water, and all my bones are out of joint;
my heart is like wax; it is melted within my breast;
my mouth is dried up, and my tongue sticks to my jaws;
you lay me in the dust of death.
My God, my God, why have you abandoned me?

I know Dad didn't realize it, and neither did I as a child, but he was singing my song, the verses written all those centuries ago by a psalmist speaking to a primal wound. I don't mean to speak blasphemy, but Jesus doesn't get to claim abandonment as his own. In some way and at some point, we have all been left, like Mike Erpelding in his trailer that Christmas he died; like Leonard that Christmas with me. My dad sang Psalm 22 to God, but he sang it to me, too, and somewhere inside me, even as a little girl, I knew it.

But just as with Leonard and all my ESLD patients in the ICU, I had the information but couldn't weave it into my conscious, daily life. Maybe I was in denial. Maybe I was trying to survive. For so long I couldn't see when my biological past rose to the surface and manifested in my present, like Blanche seeing Jesus the Christ on those red, rocky mountains. I pushed forward on the timeline of my life and went along with the socially accepted adoption script: all's well that ends well. But Leonard, my own Jesus doppelgänger, had come to renew my faith—not in the Christian sense of salvation, but as the closest I'd come to tending the suffering and death of my own biological father.

I moved into my new apartment in San Antonio two days after Christmas, just months after I'd established contact with Uncle Greg. Soon after I settled in, he sent me a care package that included a pair of photo CDs. One was labeled Miscellaneous Pics, the other, Funeral.

Greg and Christine had prepared a photo collage of Mike's life for his memorial service just two years before, so I fired up the Funeral disc first, eager to see if I looked anything like my father. With a double-click, photos of Mike began to swim across the screen, with Ozzy Osborne's tinny voice singing "See You on the Other Side" in the background.

Though I had imagined that the Erpelding ancestors, much like the Ohlmanns, had settled in Nebraska with the flood of European homesteaders toward the end of the nineteenth century, one difference between our families became immediately clear: this generation of Erpeldings was not Lutheran.

I paused on a picture. Mike sat at a kitchen table, a baby with a bottle tucked into his arms. He looked healthy, young, maybe late thirties, with brown hair, a mustache, and a western-style plaid shirt with pearled snaps for buttons. Behind him a clock on a side table showed ten o'clock, and judging by the soft light on the walls, it was morning. Mike gazed down at the baby, a can of Old Milwaukee next to him on the table.

I fixated on that photo. I downloaded it, and for weeks I looked at it first thing when I woke up and last thing before sleep. I memorized every detail and began to dream about it—not in fluid, narrative dreams but in moments where I was part of the scene in the photo, sitting at the table with Mike or watching him from the next room. After a month of near obsession, I called Greg to see if I could glean any information about the photo.

"Uncle Greg, can you tell me about a photo from Mike's funeral collage?" I asked, describing the photograph in detail.

"I'm pretty sure that's Chelsey or Shawn, Chris's boy," he said.

"It's not his baby?"

"Oh no. He had a baby girl when he was married, but she was barely home. Born premature and spent most of her life in the hospital."

"I guess I forgot he had a daughter. I didn't know she was sick."

"She didn't breathe too well, and once they got her home, she woke with a fever one morning and was dead before suppertime."

I didn't respond.

"Mike never got over that," he said. "Think he got a DUI on her birthday for three or four years after that. Sad, all Mike ever wanted was a daughter. Just his luck he had one and never knew it."

Leonard's private Christmas concert stood in stark contrast to the holiday singing disaster I'd survived the year before. In the midst of my move from New York to Texas via Nebraska, I thought it'd be a great idea to sing a solo at St. John on Christmas morning. I had sung at my childhood church every time I'd come home since the mid-1990s, so why would it be any different in the midst of a gigantic life-career-time-zone-culture-shock change that took place over the stress-free holidays and involved thousands of miles of driving in a fifteen-passenger van with two cats, a piano, and my parents, also during the same year I had established contact with both sides of my biological family? What could possibly go wrong?

On Christmas morning I glanced over at the choir from my seat at the edge of the balcony. Miss Mielke, my second grade teacher, now eighty years old and long retired, caught my eye and flashed a smile.

"Oh, Suzy, I just love when you come home and sing. God has truly blessed you," she'd enthused before the service, pulling me into one of her hugs—the same life-sustaining hugs she'd given all her students at the end of each school day back when I came up to her waist.

I smiled back and scanned the bulletin. I'd already sung a brief Psalm verse to a church filled to capacity, my hands ice cold, my voice shaky and uprooted. My big solo would come after the sermon. I kept wiping my hands on my skirt and scrambled to find an escape plan. Maybe I could pass a note to the choir director and tell him that I'd gone home sick and couldn't finish the service.

When the sermon began, I slipped down the balcony steps, through the narthex, and to the hallway by Miss Mielke's old classroom. I entered the girl's bathroom, the same one I used in second grade, with the same fluorescent lights, the wall and floor tiles a tired, institutional beige. A new soap dispenser was mounted between the two porcelain sinks, replacing the old, lamp-like vessel that held bubblegum-pink soap when I was a child.

This was the bathroom in which I had barfed one afternoon when I was supposed to be in Miss Mielke's reading group, young enough at age seven that I didn't know if my sick feeling was of the uptown or the downtown variety. I thought downtown and then proceeded to puke directly into my yellow-flowered underpants. I peeled them off and went to rinse them, praying to Jesus that no one would come in and find me half-naked at the sink. I slipped the whole wet mess back on and limped back to the classroom, back to Miss Mielke in her seat behind the half-moon table where she hosted reading group. Even as little Justin Haines read aloud about Dick and Jane and their new cat, Puff, she recognized my panic and came quickly to gather me in her arms.

"I just threw up into my underwear," I whimpered.

"Everything's going to be okay," she whispered back.

Twenty-five years later, Christmas morning, I found myself in that same bathroom and couldn't catch my breath. The flesh on the inside of my mouth started to tingle, and my ears crinkled and popped the way they do prewretch.

A voice in my mind teased me: *Better stand up so you don't puke into your underpants.*

I made it into the toilet, a small triumph.

I exited the stall to splash water on my face, my eyes bloodshot from heaving, still trying to catch my breath. Leaning on the sink, I studied my thirty-two-year-old self in the mirror, a flushed woman staring back at me taking in rapid gulps of air. What is the deal? All I have to do is sing.

I threw up again and the voice returned: *Do you want your old teachers to see you like this and find out who you really are, a scared little baby?*

I felt like a kid on a teeter-totter whose playmate has leapt off and run away, causing his friend to crash to the ground. Where had that sunshiny, confident version of me gone? I couldn't perform without her.

And what about my teachers? Would it matter to them if they knew that I didn't believe all they had taught me anymore? That I believed that the whole doctrine of the Lutheran Church Missouri Synod is judgmental and exclusive, in direct opposition to the message of Jesus the Christ? That religious and spiritual beliefs are individual and private? That communities of faith should be open, not closed, societies? What if redemption exists in vertical time and not in this mathematical equation we of the Western world have created? What if eternal life has already begun, before us, after us, and all around us? Aren't we all dying and rising with each loss, each grief, each pain we encounter in these long days on Earth?

By the time the sermon ended, I'd taken my place by the organ to fight my way through what would be my last solo at St. John. I wanted to collapse when I finished, but I stood my ground, smiling as if I'd been present through the entire performance. No one was the wiser, not my mom and dad from their spot on the left side of the congregation, not even Miss Mielke, who made a beeline for me after the service to hug me again. "Thank you for your music."

I hugged her back. "You're welcome."

By my fourth twelve-hour night in a row with Leonard, I'd run out of holiday music, not to mention energy. As the shift wound down to the final hours, I chose one closing act in my attempt to revive his dignity, if not his life. I'd given his body, bed, and room a thorough cleansing, but his ragged hairstyle remained—a mullet, the "business in the front, party in the back" look made famous by Billy Ray Cyrus in the 1990s, though it had been worn by guys and gals alike since the 1970s (Carol Brady on The Brady Bunch, Rod Stewart, David Bowie, Joe Elliot, my brother Jeff in high school). We called it "hockey hair" at St. Olaf. Leonard's mullet had become a rat's nest at the back of his neck, tangled in his dressing and stuck to the ties that anchored his tracheostomy tube.

So I climbed up onto the stool I'd been using to reach Leonard on his high-tech air bed and cut it. I found out later I needed a physician's order for such a thing, and thanks to a good-humored pulmonologist, I got one after the fact. ("Okay to trim mullet for hygienic reasons," he wrote.)

As I stepped back to admire my work, I noticed Leonard's right eye open under the soft, clear tape I used to close his eyelids every two hours. I moved in to peel the tape back, and as I tugged at it gently, his eyelid flinched.

"Leonard? Did you just blink your eye?" I pulled the last edge of tape from his cheek.

No response. I held my breath as I peeled the tape off of his left eye. He flinched again.

"Leonard? Can you hear me?"

No response.

"Leonard, if you can hear me, I want you to concentrate and try to blink one or both eyes."

After a long minute, he winked his right eye.

"Leonard?"

He winked his left.

"Leonard!" I started shaking his bed. "Are you winking at me?"

Night shift speeds quickly into day on an intensive care unit, and you hope nothing disastrous occurs between 4:30 and 6:30 a.m. as you pine to end your shift in peace, not in the scuttle of a cardiac arrest or spontaneous hemorrhage. But Leonard had other plans. After forty days of sepsis and metabolic coma, at 4:30 a.m. Leonard decided to open his eye under the tape and wink on command, the flirt. Nurses came running from all ends of the unit, unsure why my singing had changed from sacred music to shouting.

"He woke up! He woke up! Leonard! Woke! Up!" I hollered, dancing a jig around his bed.

When his pulmonologist, Dr. Ball, arrived at 5:00 a.m., I waved in maniacal semaphore from inside Leonard's room for him to join me at the bedside. A tall, stern man, not humorless but never goofy, he donned his gown and gloves in silence. Twenty-five years of critical care medicine had taught him to lower his expectations.

"Leonard," I said, "can you wink for Dr. Ball?"

He obliged, first the right eye, then the left, making us wait a split second longer for the left side—comic timing from a nearly dead man.

"Well," Dr. Ball cleared his throat. "Good we ordered that haircut, Suzanne."

I cringed, unsure Leonard would like his new do. "Uh, Leonard—I hope you don't mind, but I cut your hair. You were starting to look like Jesus."

At Christmas a year after Leonard's resurrection, he sent me a card in the mail with this message written inside:

Miss Hollywood (Suzanne),

I cannot thank you enough for the mental stimulation that your lovely voice gave me to bring me back from that place I was (which is still a mystery!) You were a beautiful sight to wake up to with a beautiful voice. I'll never be able to explain the joy you've given me by bringing me back to my family. The enclosed photo is of me and my two daughters.

    Thanks again!
    Leonard

I dug the photo out of the envelope and found Leonard with his arms around two very happy-looking girls. He had brown hair and a mustache, and he wore a western-style shirt with pearled snaps for buttons. Good health had transformed him from the look of the Lord to an even higher status in my Book of Life. Leonard, his beloved daughters in tow, was a doppelgänger for my dad.

# 9

## *Bapa*

A month after Christmas, about the time Leonard was fixing to return home to his girls, I chose to return to India, to the village where I'd decided to become a nurse and to the wizened old man who'd adopted me as his American daughter. Just over a year into my new life of nursing in San Antonio, thoughts of my next adventure had begun to manifest, a tugging sensation I knew well. If I had plotted my adult life on a map, it would have appeared as a series of migrations over great distances, like the flight of sandhill cranes, who travel eight to ten thousand miles each year from their winter nests to their summer breeding grounds. I was born in Grand Island, Nebraska, during the height of the cranes' annual roost on the Platte River, the hospital just eight miles north of the river's braided channels and most probably within earshot of the cranes' rattling cries as they flew over. What do we inherit from our birthplace—in my case, from thousands of ancient birds darkening the dawn and dusk sky in massive, wheeling numbers during the first days of my life?

Maybe they taught me to fly, to see the world beyond just one, familiar horizon. Maybe I have the cranes to thank for the flight pattern of my life, from Nebraska to Minnesota, then to New York, and finally to India, more than eight thousand miles from home, a place I would stay for three long visits, the first two before nursing school, the last soon after Leonard's awakening.

Just west of another braided river, the Devi, sits the tiny village of Juanga, my Indian destination in the eastern state of Odisha. When describing our entry into this lifetime, we say that we "were born." But people in Odisha say that a person "takes birth," a phrase introduced to me by a cheerful surgeon I assisted in Juanga's village hospital. He spoke excellent English with a thick accent. He'd been praising my efforts to learn Odia, the local language. "We are all so thrilled to hear you sing our language," he said.

"Thank you," I said. "But sing?"

"Yes. Your voice is like a bird when you speak Odia, like a *sua*."

"What is a *sua*?"

"A parrot! A songbird. We believe you took birth here in Odisha in a past lifetime, and so, on the inside, you are still a daughter of India. You are our *sua*."

My aunt Irene took birth in India, her parents Lutheran missionaries on the southern tip of the continent, so I grew up around her stories, sepia India photographs, and carved rosewood elephant tables. I adored (and still do) my auntie, and because of her, India inhabited a floating, perpetual dream space in my mind and became a place I was determined to visit.

I met a musician once, a bass player from Cameroon, a proud lion of a man with tall cheekbones framed in the rich, dark tones of his face and a set of teeth that gleamed like sunshine on a swimming pool each time he sang or smiled or spoke. We met between sets at the Jazz Standard on East Twenty-Seventh Street in New York, he the star of the show, I a friend of a friend of the star with an open seat next to me. He sat down to eat a quick dinner and studied me while I beamed back at him. His presence surprised me, my every antenna up from his performance. The tunes in his first set ranged from Jaco Pastorius's "Liberty City" to a tender Cameroonian lullaby. He had gone from dominating his instrument to singing in a soft, falsetto voice to suddenly appearing at my side to devour a burger and fries before his next set.

"You are a healer," he said between bites, his words tinged with both French and Duala, his native tongue.

I smiled, unsure what the hell he was talking about. It was 2002, I was twenty-six years old, and it was my second year in New York. My days were attuned to music as a career, my nights filled with worry about doing more for society than just singing.

"You are a singer, a good singer, but healing will come to you."

Was it wrong to believe him just because he was exotic and spoke with a French-African accent? To assume he knew some secret of the earth that I didn't because I grew up in Nebraska and he in a sub-Saharan village? I believed his every word, but perhaps I was under the spell of his music or the gin and tonic I'd been sipping or the sight of his fingers sliding up and down the neck of his five-string, fretless bass.

I didn't tell him I'd been a bass player myself or that I'd played the Guns N' Roses tune "Welcome to the Jungle" before varsity basketball games at Seward High School. I was tongue-tied by his proclamations and also sure that when he asked me to go home with him after the show, I would say yes. (And I did.)

"Tell me something: if you could go anywhere in the world, where would you go?" he asked.

"India," I said.

"India," he nodded, mouth full of fries. "Good choice."

I grinned. I was ready to marry him.

"India has a smell like no other place in the world," he said. "You'll see when you go. And someday," he said, leaning so close that I could feel his breath on my lips, "you will go."

Oh, how right he was.

Three full years into my New York migration, my longing for India peppered my daily thoughts. Ever since the September 11 attacks just two weeks after I arrived in the city, I worried about my lack of helpful skills; the pragmatism of my upbringing played a loud second fiddle to my artistic pursuits. I'd ride the subway to my job as artistic advisor of the Eos Orchestra and daydream about volunteering in India. During the sermons at my weekly church singing gig, I'd brainstorm lists of jobs on the service folder, from massage therapist to psychoanalyst to physician. By the end of each sermon, I'd have crossed off every option but nursing.

When Eos began to struggle and finally closed its doors, I flew to India to volunteer at a rural NGO hospital and school. I flew from JFK through Kuwait City on December 26, 2004, with a window seat over the Iraq war and a view past Baghdad and smoke plumes. The tsunami hit Indonesia and India the day I flew, and news coverage was broadcast on televisions throughout the small Kuwait City airport, but I was too bleary-eyed to watch TV and also too taken with the Arab men and their head gear, hundreds of them in suits and ties and red and white head wraps called *keffiyeh*. The airport gifted me with the most foreign-feeling hours of my life, camped as I was with my new layover friends, a young Pakistani couple on route to Lahore, as I waited to fly to Delhi.

The NGO's director, Michael, whom I'd met through my work at Eos, picked me up in Delhi. He'd been running the project for more than ten years, and he guided me, jet-lagged and culture-shocked, through auto-rickshaw rides, beggar children with missing fingers in traffic jams, a textile market, and a warm plate of paneer masala before bed. A rancid smell followed us through Delhi: stale urine, cow dung, burning trash, a new and foul combination of odors. In the morning we boarded the Rajdhani Express to cross India, a thirty-six-hour train ride from Delhi to Bhubaneswar in Odisha, a state on the east coast, just south of West Bengal (home to Kolkata) and just north of the tsunami's devastation in Andhra Pradesh.

I slept, and when I was awake, I drank approximately one hundred cups of chai.

I squatted to pee over an open hole on the moving train and watched the urine drip onto the tracks beneath, bracing myself on stained lavatory walls while the bathroom door slammed open and closed behind me. It smelled bad. I wanted to plug my nose, but I couldn't spare a hand or I'd fall through the pee hole.

I wanted to close my eyes to the bright saris, to the wandering cows, to the burning trash piles, to the torn Bollywood posters on stained city walls, to the long stares from packs of Indian men on the station platform, to the shanty towns and urban slums, to the dead dogs on the side of the road. I wanted to plug my ears to the barrage of noise, the loud careening buses with their shrieking, elephant-call horns; the motorcycles and auto rickshaws honking and zigzagging around slow-moving ox carts with their tired, barefoot owners; the vendors shouting at fried food stalls; and the chai wallahs wandering up and down the length of the train, calling, "Chai, madam, chai, chai, chai, chai!"

This was not the India I had imagined through Irene's stories, pictures, and elephant tables. Irene took birth in India, and decades later she married my Uncle Bob, little brother of Pat, mother of me, though I took birth in Grand Island from a different mother. By fate or faith or divine intervention, Irene became my aunt and my godmother, and she inspired me to choose India. Her love and presence reminded me that the arrow of my life had always been pointing to that chaotic, mystical place, even when I had my mind on other adventures.

I prefer village life to the cities in India; it's more quiet, there's less unauthorized burning, and there are fewer stinging smells and crowds of staring men. During my first visit, once Michael left me—the sole American living and working among the local Juanga staff, a few with a bit of English, but most not—I found my greatest struggle was an internal battle of wills, half of me overcome with culture shock and discomfort, constantly crafting an escape plan, the other half enraged at my inability to cope.

I discovered that if I dictated what I was seeing in the midst of the experience, a sort of play-by-play of my adventure, the jarring feelings eased their grip. Safe in the world of foreign birdcalls, Kirtan music (the religious music of both Odisha and West Bengal dating back to the sixteenth century), and the bouncing, animated vowels of the Odia language, I could narrate my experience audibly and not offend a soul.

"I'm looking at a woman with a baby outside the hospital, and now she's holding it up and away from her and, whoops, yes, it is peeing right there in the waiting area because it has no diaper, no pants, no nothing, and it seems to be wearing black eyeliner."

"A little boy is pooping right there by the side of the road. He's making eye contact with me now, and he's pooping, and I'm walking past and he's still pooping."

"Folks, the old hospital doctor is eating his dinner and farting as he eats. Loud, blustery butt blasts. An '1812 Overture' of gas. Just another Tuesday in Juanga."

"Hello, cockroach. I see you and your other three-inch friends. Just because I am squatting over this hole to pee and it seems like you have access does not mean I'm going to let you crawl inside my vagina. Are we clear?"

Despite my monologues, I was painfully aware that I was the only person in the entire region sent reeling by power outages (constant), cold, bucket showers (no electricity, no electric water pump, no pump, no filling of the tank, no water in the tank, no overhead shower—and don't even ask about hot water), and left-handed wiping. (For those of you unaware, India is, generally speaking, a toilet-paper-free zone. In fact, our idea of a commode does not compute in rural India. If you are lucky, you will use a latrine that has two porcelain foot grips on either side of a hole over which you, the user, will squat to do your business. Next to this contraption, as you squat and try to maintain your balance—because you have not squatted for this length of time since you were three years old and building castles with blocks—you will find a large bucket filled with water of questionable cleanliness. Floating in this water is a smaller bucket that you are to use to scoop water out of the big bucket. You must then find a way to splash that water onto your sacred environs in lieu of the aforementioned toilet paper. Any manual interaction with said water or soiled body parts during this "cleansing" process is to be done with your left hand only, which is why the right hand is reserved for eating—a manual process performed sans utensils and yet another source of culture shock—as well as writing, shaking of other hands, and so on.) No, the poor of Juanga did not teach me about happiness (how exhausting is the rhetoric about poor people being happier?) or the glory of their simple lives. There's nothing simple about one meal a day or watering down your children's milk to make it last longer.

I traveled to Juanga with a twofold plan: to find out if I wanted to become a nurse by assisting in the hospital and to teach a group of so-called Third World strangers something helpful from the so-called First World, like proper hand hygiene and the importance of sex education to prevent the spread of HIV. But only after six weeks of mind games and loneliness and the frantic slathering on of mosquito-repelling, malaria-preventing cream at night, followed by an obsessive mosquito-net-tucking ritual, only to wake with the urge to pee at 3:00 a.m. and thus undo the cocoon and climb out of my wooden bed, grab the kerosene lantern, tiptoe downstairs past the sleeping security guard and his shotgun and the patients unable to sleep due to pain or hunger, and cross through the yard and into the latrine and the company of those three-inch cockroaches—only after six weeks of hearing the voice of Jack Nicholson in *A Few Good Men* shouting "You can't handle Juanga!"—did I give up my plan and finally surrender to my surroundings.

It's not easy to let go of plans. Just ask my mother, a woman whose plans for her entire life are written on recycled scraps of paper ("I do not wish my legacy on this earth to be a large pile of garbage, Suzanne"), none of which include trips to rural India or adventures in foreign toilet hygiene. My struggle to let go in Juanga made me feel like I'd brought my mother with me. I could have stuck to my initial Juanga plan. I could have stayed in my head, doused my hands in Purell, and counted the minutes until I could return to the land of flush toilets and hot showers. But what would happen if I started listening more than I talked to myself, even if it meant listening to a language I didn't understand? What if I was there for something I hadn't actually planned? What if my life's biggest leap had more to teach me than I could conceive of on my own?

I first let go a month after I arrived in Juanga. A hospital employee's mother had died, and the staff was invited to the final celebration ritual that takes place on the fourteenth day after a death. It was evening, pitch black outside, early February, and a group of us walked together with flashlights (snakes are always a danger, and these aren't bull snakes or even rattlers; we're talking king cobra) on narrow footpaths through lentil and peanut fields to the grieving family's compound of mud huts. I wrapped myself in a wool shawl that I bought with Michael at that Delhi textile market during my first days in India and listened to the chatter of my coworkers, wondering what the hell that racket was blaring over loud speakers that seemed to get louder and louder as we approached the house.

As soon as I arrived, I nearly tripped over a generator that provided power to a circle of fluorescent tube lights and a cluster of gnarled-out speakers. The lights illuminated a group of twenty-five to thirty village men singing and drumming, sitting in an oval formation on a large sheet of worn plastic tarp. I stopped still, transfixed by the raw nature of the music, not to mention the frayed wiring that powered the sound and lighting system. I'd never heard these rhythms, never seen such a spectacle, never knew that the shirtless men I'd seen carrying giant bales of rice stalks tied to the ends of a bamboo rod over their shoulders, each bale the size of a Smart car, could transform into these powerful, even possessed, musicians.

"These are the musicians," I said, my voice inaudible in the din, not one person in our group concerned by my mouth breathing. "These are my people."

The men on the inner ring of the group sat with two-sided drums the size of watermelons on their laps, pounding away, some singing along, as a tall man, the leader, paced and sang in the midst of them, a microphone hanging on a thread above him. He wore a white Punjabi shirt (a knee-length, button-down shirt with a Nehru collar), a white dhoti (a large, cotton cloth fashioned around the waist to create the look of genie pants or, more twentieth century, MC Hammer pants;

Gandhi always wore a dhoti made from cotton he'd spun into thread himself), and a vivid, magenta scarf around his neck. He sang in guttural, shouting tones, his hands gesticulating, and a small group of the men in the oval sang in response to his message. It was like storytelling with a backup group, like preaching in a gospel church where the congregation responds to the preacher and is liable to break into song at any moment.

The tall man in white, still singing, picked up a pair of cymbals the size of dinner plates and started clanging them together in rhythm with his song, pacing the length of the group. As he passed by, each drummer looked up and shouted syllables I couldn't decipher at him, as if they were counting. The singer leaned down and the drummers pounded harder, shouting back at him, trying to cut him off, trying to end the song, a competition to cut each other off with shouts and flailing gestures.

Finally there was something louder than my own thoughts: music to resurrect the music within me.

The grieving family grabbed me and hustled me into the house with the hospital staff to sit and eat and drink chai, but I couldn't focus on anything, not the fried bread called *puri*, the lentil stew called *dalma*, the plate of finger-sized bananas called *kadali*, or the fact that they'd served me a cup of chai with pure, undiluted milk straight from their cow. They were grieving their mother's death by treating me like royalty, and I was halfway out the door, gawking at the musicians. I homed in on the oldest drummer in the circle—an ancient, prune-like man, bald but for a few wispy patches, teeth like a dropped box of drill bits, as old a man as I'd ever seen in person—pounding away, screaming at the singer, yanking his arthritic hand up toward the singer's face to cut him off, confident he'd ended the song on the right beat, and then kvetching to himself when the singer passed him and tested the next drummer down.

The next day I nearly tripped over this same ancient drummer as he napped on the porch outside my classroom. He'd been cultivating pumpkins in the field next to the school and decided it was time for a rest. Once he woke and recognized me, he spoke in a low, raspy voice through the animated interpretations of the hospital's best translator.

"I saw the way you watched and counted the music last night. You can do all the work you want in the hospital, but I know you are a musician and I'm going to teach you our music. Come find me under that tree when I'm done in my field and you with your work."

So I found the ancient drummer. We sat under a tree on the edge of the pond just down from the hospital, the sun drooping in the west, farmers all around us ending their day, leading cows home, carrying the last bundles of peanuts and pumpkins on their shoulders. He spoke and I mimicked his hands, tapping out long, rhythmic songs on the sides of my knees, each song made up of syllables, each syllable a certain tap or touch on the two-sided drum I had watched him play, called a *mrdanga*. The only thing I can compare this *kirtan* method to is the solfège technique in Western music, in which notes of the scale are assigned a certain syllable, like *do*, *re*, and *mi*, and then a sequence of notes is learned by knowing the sequence of syllables.

He taught me one such series, or mantra, and after a few tries, I repeated it back to him. He taught me another mantra and I repeated it. On the third he started shouting to anyone walking past: Pinku, the teenager running the chai shop across from us; Benua, the water buffao herdsman tying his four beasts to their posts for the night; Nounidi, one of the ancient drummer's few contemporaries in Juanga, though he didn't look nearly as old—less stooped, thicker hair, fewer missing teeth. He called them over to listen while I sounded out the long string of syllables in repeated verses he'd just taught me. Each bent down to listen with rapt attention and then burst into knee-slapping laughter when I finished. I didn't know what I was doing, but there was obvious entertainment value that filled my cup and then some. I'd also developed a major elder-crush on this geezer drummer and his ridiculously long femur bones, his bulging, arthritic knees, his calloused hands, and his fingers puffed out like grapes in the top digits, maybe from drumming.

He stopped me and his voice softened, his eyes twinkling and his tiny, round head bobbing back and forth as he spoke. Then he bumped his palm into my forehead twice, saying something like "Bah-go-bahn," which I later learned meant *God*.

"What's he saying?" I asked Pinku, one of the few Juangans who understood my brief, English questions.

"Blessing from the God, sister," Pinku smiled, the old man still talking. "First saying God's name," he said, stopping to listen, "and now asking that you are calling him Bapa, because you are not a stranger, you are his daughter."

"*Bapa* means 'father'?" I asked.

"Yes," Pinku said, the ancient drummer bobbing faster in agreement.

"Okay," I said, unable to join in the head movement (how do they do that?). I shook my head instead. I'd left New York and music and flew to the other side of the earth from my birthplace in Nebraska with specific goals to accomplish and clear questions in mind, and instead I was being adopted by a musician. This was not my plan. I pressed my hands together over my heart in a silent namaste and said, "You are my Bapa, okay?"

"Okay, okay," Bapa smiled, the only English I would ever hear him speak.

I let go on my second India visit by falling in love with an unavailable Hare Krishna—unavailable due to the vows of chastity he had taken until marriage, which made him, according to his religious practice, a *brahmachari* (a celibate). There was simply no way the cultural differences could ever have been bridged, and he knew that. He just wanted to dabble in the arms of an open-hearted Nebraskan, and I, as previously established, had mastered the art of loving the wrong people.

He was a member of the sect of Hinduism most recognizable in the Western world, ISKCON, the International Society of Krishna Consciousness, and ran an internet café in Puri, one of Odisha's larger cities, where I'd often go to check email and take a break from village work.

I'd silently wept in his café on multiple occasions throughout my first India visit, overcome with homesickness in the soft, pink walls of his clean, air-conditioned space, sandalwood incense burning at the Radha and Krishna altar in one corner, the ghazals of Jagjit Singh playing on a constant, meditative loop. The chaos of an Indian city passed by, but his shop, the Halla Gulla (Hindi for "noise," an ironic name considering the peaceful environment he curated), seemed almost immune to it, but for the power outages. I arrived at age thirty for my second India visit in January of 2007, chucked my flip-flops outside the shop door, and practically leaped into my friend's arms, immediately aware that the sight of him had inspired more than a platonic reaction within me.

His religious practice required him to shave his head but for a tuft of hair at the crown called a *sikha*, a constant reminder of the vows of brahmachari he had taken, but sometimes he let the rest of his hair grow long enough that you almost forgot about it. Maybe that was the point. My focus during my Puri visits shifted from email correspondence to my friend's broad smile, his ready laughter, his body's slight scent of sweet masala, and the plates of his mother's freshly made curries and rice and chapatis he brought me to eat, along with papaya and banana from his uncle's garden next door and green coconut water and rich ginger chai.

For my birthday he gave me a little party in the yoga studio next door and served *prasad*—a variety of food prepared as an offering to God, with extra rich ingredients like coconut milk and clarified butter—made by the priests at the Jagannath Temple, India's third holiest site. Though we ate with a small group of his friends, he and I shared a plate and he fed me each bite by hand. He was beginning to become my brahmachari.

On my next Puri visit, he welcomed Bapa when I brought him with me from the village, and we happily drummed an afternoon away on the floor of his shop. Bapa even suggested we get married, and he offered Shiva, his milk cow, as dowry.

For his birthday he again brought *prasad* from the temple, and the feeding practice continued, with me waiting for each bite like a baby bird, his fingers lingering longer and longer at my lips, until I knew his brahmachari oaths had begun to fade. From that moment my visits to Puri increased from monthly to biweekly, and I stopped staying at the hotel down the road and instead stayed at his uncle's hostel, where my room was across the garden from the apartment he shared with his mother and younger brother.

I'm sure his mother knew. What mom doesn't hear her son leaving his bed in the night, whether for a drink of water or an extended violation of his religious vows? She was always friendly, but she spoke no English and my Odia had not expanded enough to say, "Say, I'm talking with your son about crazy things like a Hindu wedding and splitting time between America and India. Just what you'd always planned, I'm sure. Namaste." We thought we'd fallen in love, though now I cringe at the affair. He was a good friend, handsome and funny, and he gave me comfort in a completely foreign environment. But did we really have to get naked?

Over the course of our four-month courtship, twice he surprised me with a visit to Juanga, his scarves flying in the wind as he wound around the last curve of the hospital lane on his Hero Honda motorcycle, *sikha* adrift on his head, a pair of large Bollywood sunglasses on his face. This embarrassed me. I couldn't help but wonder if he was pronouncing himself above the country folk of the village, consciously or otherwise, despite the fact that they shared the same language, religion, statehood, and nationality.

On his second surprise visit, Bapa and I were en route to play kirtan for a fourteen-day funeral gathering in a neighboring village. My brahmachari boyfriend joined us and gestured for me to ride with him on his motorcycle. Bapa nodded, but when I hopped onto the seat, he stared in disgust as we sped on. I should have ridden sidesaddle, like all the other women in India.

Disgust evolved into resignation as we sat at the drumming circle and my brahmachari walked around us, snapping photos with his camera, then his phone, and then his second phone. The funeral was for the mother of a fellow drummer, and I nearly threw up when he approached me between the music and the meal to ask if my "friend" was from Odisha—no local boy could have acted so rudely.

The final blow came when we'd reached the ending moments of our communal dinner. The musicians, twenty or thirty in number, sat on the ground in a large semicircle and ate supper off banana leaves. Members of the grieving family served us from buckets of boiled rice, lentil stew, tomato chutney, and sweet rice pudding—my favorite. Whenever it came time for the rice pudding, all the musicians, knowing how I loved it, would encourage me to eat more, shouting at me the command form of the verb *kaiba* (to eat). "Suzanni! Kah! Kah!"

The custom at these meals is to slurp your way through the food, eating hand to mouth in rapid, swooping motions. All other noises are allowed as well—belching, farting, throat clearing, snot rockets—but when the slurping begins to decrescendo, you should look up and assess the status of your fellow eaters. When all are finished, and more than once these kind men waited for me, only then do you rise as a group and walk to the water pump to rinse off. But not my brahmachari. When he had had his fill, he stood, beckoned the grieving family to bring him some water, and made a series of phone calls.

This silenced the crowd, and all eyes were on me. I bowed my head in shame. Bapa shouted a gruff "What the hell are you looking at?" in my defense, then nudged me with his elbow and said, "Kah." Eat.

Jesus the Christ, if the dude couldn't act respectful toward my Juanga family, how would he react to a game of Polish rummy in Nebraska? And why hadn't I thought of that before I let him feed me all that sensual God food?

At the very least, I can say that my brahmachari didn't break my heart. That night I chose not to lecture him on proper village manners—that would be a puzzling message from a foreign visitor to a native Odishan—but I did ask him to stop making visits to Juanga. When he asked why, I told him I could never love him more than I loved my village family. If India had become home, I would live not in Puri or at his Halla Gulla but in the village, dust on my feet, Bapa yelling at me from his potato field. True to his devout faith and my mercurial temperament, we had one last romp in the wee hours of the next morning, and he left the village at sunrise.

It was Bapa who made me cry when I'd leave him. We both cried, so much so that he insisted on accompanying me to the airport the first time I left Juanga, and he said he hadn't cried that hard since he'd given his daughters away at the time of their marriage.

"Then why do you want me to get married?" I cried, beside myself.

"Hey!" he'd shout and then rattle off some diatribe about how no matter where we live in the world, we aren't meant to be alone—all this while wiping tears from my face with his *gamcha* (a hand towel no Indian farmer is without, similar to a handkerchief the size of a dish towel, most often worn around the neck but also used as head wrap, turban, towel, belt, dust rag, and soft whip for ornery cows and, most impressive, tied quickly into impromptu swimming trunks by children on the banks of India's rivers).

"But I am alone," I'd howl into a new chorus of sobs.

People in the village loved to tease me about Bapa's mortality. Often I'd pass the temple on the way to his house, groups of men gathered there to rest in the afternoon breeze and play cards, and some random farmer half-asleep on his *gamcha* would shout, "Your Bapa's not home!" *Bapa ghara nahee!*

"Why?" I'd stop and ask. *Kahinki?*

"Dead!" he'd shout back, and the crowd would erupt in laughter. *Marigola!*

On countless occasions, and I do not exaggerate, six to eight of us musicians would be walking to a neighboring village—Bapa at the rear with his giant, bamboo walking stick and hurried, almost mechanical gait (picture bowed, toothpick legs with grapefruit-sized knees taking steps a yard at a time, and fast)—and someone would say, "Suzanni, Tume Bapa kwade?" *Where's your Bapa?*

"Bapa achunti!" I'd say. *He's right here!* Then I'd turn around to find someone pseudo-strangling him. Sometimes Mohan, the village milkman, whose laugh beats Santa Claus when it comes to jolly, would toss Bapa over his shoulder like a sack of potatoes. Other times he would hoist him up to ride piggyback. These are not common sights between friends, family, and the elderly in America. But most American elders don't spend their days cultivating lentils and ground peanuts by hand so their grandchildren can eat. At age 969 (the age of Methusaleh), Bapa was stronger and more flexible than I was at thirty, and he laughed until his eyes were wet at my shocked reaction to the elder-hazing.

But on my third trip to Juanga, Bapa contracted a vicious strain of malaria. This time I was thirty-three, on leave from my intensive care job in San Antonio, with thoughts of Leonard's Christmas resurrection still fresh in my mind. I had believed that this trip would convince me to sell my earthly possessions and dive into the migrant life of international health work. But again my ideas began to morph in the tired hands of my Bapa, Juanga's oldest drummer.

Each evening at dusk, I walked to the tea hut down the road from the hospital and sat and drank chai with a group of farmers who'd brought in their harvest for the night and wanted to mumble a few words to each other about the day. These men reminded me of farmers from my childhood: hard hands, sore backs, spare in the description of their work. One night, knowing Bapa was ailing and thinking I'd want to know, they described for me in detail all that would happen if and when he died. I cried at the image of his tiny body being cleansed and anointed, then wrapped in white cloth, then burned that same day at the temple. One man, Benua, whom I'd nicknamed Moisi Raja (King of the Water Buffaloes), saw my sadness and kindly changed the subject, asking me what I'd been doing to care for Bapa in these last days. As I began to describe my nursing routine, I found a captive audience in these men, with their walking sticks, evening shawls, and bare, calloused feet.

I told them that Bapa was too sick to come to the hospital, so I'd been taking him his medication three times a day, following the shortcut from the hospital over dusty foot paths, through clumps of palm and banana trees, past a water pump and three naked village children splashing through their morning bath, past an old woman in a tattered sari bent down to sweep a yard of dried mud and dust into brilliant, curving swaths, and into the mud stable where I'd find him, moaning and wracked with fever on the cool dirt floor of his cow house. This is where he rests, I told them, in the company of Shiva and Parvati, his beloved milk cows.

When I pinched the skin on Bapa's hand, it stayed in place—tenting, a sign of dehydration. I shone a penlight into his eyes, his pupils equal and reactive to light. Heat radiated off his face and neck and head. The pulse at his wrist felt rapid and thready, that of an old heart in a long fight. I wanted to pick him up, throw him over my shoulder, and run to the hospital so I could start an IV and fill him with fluids, pain medication, and sedatives to help him sleep. I wanted to hook him up to a heart monitor and create my own little intensive care unit right there in Juanga, draw labs to check his electrolytes, swab his mouth with ice water, and cover his cracked lips with balm.

"Jhia, mori jibi?" he asked, his voice barely audible. *Little daughter, am I dying?*

"Na, Bapa, aji nahi." *No, Dad, not today.*

"Tu muara jhia." *You are my daughter.*

"Apana muara Bapa." *And you my Bapa.*

I didn't want him to die. I had come to rural India to find out if I wanted to become a nurse. Then I'd come again in the midst of nursing school. And then again after working years on an intensive care unit. And though my questions about my career were initially answered, I believed Bapa answered a greater question about my very existence, and he had done so every time we'd spoken, including the first, when he said, "Tu muara jhia." *You are my daughter.* He was a cranky old codger, bent at the waist and full of the expertise and opinions known to geezers the world 'round. But when he told me I was his daughter, his eyes crinkled, and without fail, he would reach out his hand, brown, leathery, and callused from a lifetime of manual farming on the plains of rural Odisha, and bless me, tapping the cracked skin of his palm against my forehead, a smile tugging at the corners of his mouth. It was as if I'd asked him for this. It was as if I'd asked him to love me like his own. It was as if I asked this wherever I went.

I passed through the courtyard where his daughter-in-law squatted over the fire, boiling milk for chai, lines of concern etched across her forehead. "Courtyard" suggests a grandeur that didn't exist at Bapa's house, though he and his family did actually sleep in a cinder block structure they built with government aid after the 1999 super cyclone decimated their former mud hut. They used the house for sleeping and the courtyard and covered porch for living, the women crouched over the cooking fire at meal time, the children barefoot and tearing up the village paths, and Bapa, when in good health, shifting from work in the field to meals in the courtyard, then a nap on a teak wood bed inside, then late afternoon commentary sessions at the front stoop, where he offered his interpretation of the day's events to anyone who would listen and watched the slow traffic of Juanga's main drag.

But not this day. On this day I went to find his wife and we made *lembu pani*, lemon water, the only kind he would take with his pills.

She greeted me with a nod from her spot on the floor, where she was slicing tiny, green fruit across the upright-facing blade of a *paniki*, a mounted knife used in every house in the village, a tool I referred to as the Juanga Cuisinart. Before I had a chance to speak, she began telling me her plans for Bapa's death. She'd decided I would light the funeral pyre.

"Boouuu," I said, sighing over the Odia word for *mother*. "Mori jiba nahee!" *He's not dying!*

"Heck!" she shouted, smacking my arm. "Kemmti janee cha?" *How do you know?*

I was used to this gruff communication style by now, the scolding "heck" almost always accompanied by a swat, Bapa usually grabbing a shoe or his tall, bamboo walking stick and wielding it over his head.

She spoke again of his funeral rituals.

I shuddered, then gestured in silence toward the front stoop where their oldest son sat and smoked, his two most frequent activities. Bapa looked older than Methuselah and still worked harder than his son.

She bobbled her head side to side. "Suzani eko, eko." *You're his favorite.*

Shiva let out a long bellow from the cow house, the only sound to match Bapa's groans as I returned to the hut. I'd bought his family mosquito nets for malaria prevention on my last visit to Juanga, but I hadn't seen them hung on this visit. Or maybe he didn't tuck them in every night like I did when I was there. I don't know. I just wanted his fever to break and avoided the temptation to isolate any kind of root cause for his plight. He took his pills and, at my urging, choked down the rest of the *lembu pani.* I dipped a cloth in a bowl of water and wrapped his head, sure I could see steam rising from the fever. I told him I'd be back for his next dose and that I loved him, though in English—like the farmers from the plains back home, he wasn't one for flowery talk. As I rose to leave, he stretched out his hand and beckoned me back to him.

I tossed my bag on the floor and sat down again, my head at eye level with Shiva's udder. Bapa whispered a Sanskrit mantra I'd learned with him on my first visit to Juanga, a common prayer to Shiva, the god of both destruction and compassion. I often heard the chant at night in the hospital, sung by recovering patients and their visiting family members, the day darkened, the only light a single flame from an oil lamp on the floor.

"Bolo, bolo," Bapa said. *Sing for me.*

I bowed my head and chanted:

*Karpura gauraum, koruna avataraum,*
*samsara saraum, bhujagendra haraum.*
*Sadha basante, rhuduya rabinde,*
*babham babhani, sahitam namami.*

Purest white like camphor, the incarnation of compassion
The essence of worldly existence, whose garland is the king of
    serpents,

Always dwelling in the pure, lotus-like heart,
I bow to Shiva and Shakti together.

As the prayer ended, Bapa commenced his own quiet monologue. Though I couldn't decipher every word, I knew he was talking about his concerns about my marriage and how, if I'd lived in Juanga, he would have found me a good husband and provided a fruitful dowry on my behalf. This was one of Bapa's favorite topics, spoken with a twinkle in his eye, listing not only the cows and sheep he would give but also goats, chickens, cats and dogs, even water buffalo to sweeten the deal. I hushed him, but he continued, his voice low, and began to repeat one phrase. "Khojeeba tu parivara." *Find your family.* He took my hand. "Khojeeba tu parivara." *Find your family.*

Bapa thought he was dying and wanted to give me his best advice before it was too late. But he wasn't dying, and though he probably meant to encourage me to find a husband and have children, village style, his words went straight to my gut, a realization transforming me right there on the dirt floor. I could continue to travel the world and seek adoption wherever I went, or I could find my family. I could keep migrating, or I could land.

"I love you, Bapa."

I pressed his hand to my cheek and rose to leave the cow house. I walked past the water pump, the palms, and the old woman sweeping, and I reached the hospital to start my day with my fellow nurses, a line of villagers already at the front door. Bapa would survive—he'd turned the corner on the worst of the fevers. And I would land and find my family.

# 10

## Hatchet

Fifth graders can take band at St. John Lutheran School, and I had big plans to play the trumpet. But Mom, chair of the school board, had spoken with the band teacher and discovered that nobody had signed up for trombone or any kind of low brass instruments. My parents raised us as can-do, fill-in-the-gap children when it came to church and school. No acolyte showed for the 10:45 a.m. service? Suzy will do it. The New Testament reader has laryngitis? Jeff is available. No trombones in the band? Why not Suzy, even though she wants to play trumpet or flute or drums or, a close fourth place, saxophone? But I played the trombone, and that's how I found my family. Twenty-five years after my baptism into the kingdom of low brass, I married Ryan Westerhoff, a Seward boy, a trombone player, and my high school marching band section leader.

I was in seventh grade the first time I saw Ryan, a bright spot in the dimly lit, windowless, storm-shelter safety of the St. John Lutheran School cafeteria, a room transformed into a junior high dance hall by balloons, colored streamers, and a buzzing black light. An exotic ninth grader from the Public School Downtown, Ryan had come as a guest of one of our ninth grade girls. According to legend, kids from the public school mixed sloe gin with their Mountain Dew and slid right past first and second base into the hinterlands of home run territory. They knew more about sin than any of us St. John children would dare to ask.

The summer before, my dad had read the book *Hatchet*, by Gary Paulsen, to our family during our annual vacation. The book tells the story of a teenage boy and his heroic struggle to survive in the Canadian wilderness after a plane crash. The front cover of Dad's book showed an illustration of the protagonist, Brian Robeson, a handsome boy with a full head of black hair, arched black eyebrows, and a strong jawline. None of the boys at St. John looked like Hatchet. But Ryan did: the hair, the eyebrows, the full, red lips, the jaw line. I stood frozen against the wall as he entered the dance, a quiet, athletic grace encircling each step. His broad shoulders gleamed in the fluorescent light from the hallway. Tall. Corn-fed. Perfect. Where had he come from? Did his people have a name? I worried that the smell of sour milk wafting out of the cooler in the corner might pollute his experience. He deserved clean air.

My infatuated paralysis only increased when the DJ cued up the number one ballad on the Top 40 charts: "Love Bites," by Def Leppard, a slow dance. My lips began to chap from mouth breathing as I watched Ryan and his two other Public School Downtown Casanovas escort their St. John dates onto the floor. Without hesitation, those boys held the girls in a close embrace through the entire five-plus minutes of the song. One boy even put his hands in the back pockets of the Lutheran girl's jeans.

We didn't speak. He clearly had a girlfriend and would probably have one for the rest of his babe-ly life, so I didn't put all my eggs in his basket. I mean, if I had a dozen eggs, I'm pretty sure I'd put at least one out there for other Hatchet types. But there weren't any in Seward. I chased boys through junior high and high school, but from that first moment in the carpeted walls of our lunchroom, Ryan Westerhoff was it.

By sophomore year of high school, my crush had waned and I was happy with friendship. Each fall morning before school, we practiced our marching band routine, Ryan and I both in the trombone section, me the only girl, he the senior section leader. Our high school was small enough that kids could do sports and band, and Ryan, six-foot-four, lean, and muscular, also started for the football team. He arrived the Friday morning of the first game jazzed up for the team's season debut, showing off his new, sticky football gloves. During breaks I'd hold his trombone so he could practice his wide receiver routes, my beautiful friend darting from his imaginary line of scrimmage, suddenly oblivious to the band director shouting into the megaphone in the background and the clusters of flag corps girls rushing to their positions. When he let me try on his gloves, my fingers swam in their extra-large size, and that's when I noticed his hands. I was so overcome as I watched him squeeze each finger back into the gloves and snap the Velcro across the breadth of his broad, sinewy wrists that I nearly dug my trombone slide into the practice field turf. I was ruined. Those cold, fall mornings, moving in and out of our marching formations, wrote the first chapters of a book I've never put down.

It never occurred to me that I might marry a Nebraskan. I was the girl who reeled during junior year sociology class when Mr. Moody put a pie chart on the overhead projector that showed the geographical statistics of marital likelihood.

"A high percentage of you will marry someone not only from Nebraska but from Seward County," he said.

*Barf*, I thought. Ryan had dumped me, graduated, and left town. His silent departure from our romance and, even worse, from our friendship had left me devastated the year before. Sometime after Christmas of his senior year, we'd switched gears from band buddies to holding hands as we cruised downtown Seward in his white '86 LeBaron. Then he kissed me. And on our final date, we lay on the velvet, floral, orange and brown couch in his basement, fully clothed but wandering into the territory I'd been strictly taught to avoid throughout eighth and ninth grade religion class. The closer his perfect hands came to my holy of holies, the more I felt I'd stumbled into the walk-in cooler at Dairy Queen, my little, Lutheran body shivering in the icy winds of original sin. I'd worn button-fly jeans in the hopes of slowing the process, but they were no match for a wide receiver from the Public School Downtown. I kept waiting for my body to warm up and join the fun, but I couldn't. I wouldn't have known what to do but just lie there, scared and cold. When his left hand became affixed to my forehead due to copious amounts of Aquanet hairspray shellacked onto a tower of bangs (this was 1992), and then became unstuck with an awkward, audible *schluck!*, we both gave up. He drove me home, kissed me goodnight, and didn't really talk to me again that year. I knew the only way to flush him from my system would be to escape on a grand scale. Perhaps college in Minnesota, then music in New York, a few European backpacking jaunts, a change of course into nursing, and some long visits to India would be the decades-long diversion I needed to move past an old flame.

Though I didn't actually try to predict the trajectory of my life there in Mr. Moody's sociology class, I was certain Ryan would become a distant memory. Yet when we reconnected after more than fifteen years of zero contact, I felt a little pinwheel inside of me, motionless for years, start spinning again. I had just graduated from nursing school at Columbia, and he was a full-time firefighter in San Antonio. *And he was unavailable*, my specialty at the time. It seemed an impossibility then that we would do more than exchange a few emails and return to our separate lives, let alone marry. But Mr. Moody was right, and here's how it happened:

*How to Rekindle Romance with Your High School Sweetheart
When He Lives in Texas and You in New York (and He's Married)
In 32 Short Steps*

1. Do a cartwheel when your long-lost sweetheart emails you out of the blue after sixteen years.
2. Start talking on the phone every three days, but only when he's at work at the fire station.
3. He's MARRIED. He's UNHAPPILY MARRIED. Assure yourself you're not having an emotional affair, despite the way your insides tingle when you hear his voice.
4. Fly to visit him in San Antonio while his wife is away, but don't stay with him. Stay with your best friend, Guz, a gifted pianist with whom you've performed recitals at Juilliard, though you both prefer to play

songs like "Blame Canada!" and "Uncle Fucker" from the *South Park* movie. Your South Park renditions help distract you from the Dinner Date with Ryan in San Antonio, which you ask Guz to chaperone. Eat at a twenty-four-hour tourist trap chock-full of piñatas and wandering mariachis, because those blaring trumpets and screaming men in their bejeweled pantaloons distract you and your sweetheart from any kind of romantic impulse.

5. Stop talking to your sweetheart after the visit because it's too painful to be in love with another married man and you can't stand yourself anymore.

6. Fly back to San Antonio a month later to do volunteer nursing in the disaster shelters during Hurricane Ike. Sleep on Guz's couch again. You're there to help the evacuees, not to see your sweetheart, though he's moved out now and it seems okay to maybe just go have a beer with him at the Broadway 5050 bar, this time without a chaperone. He kisses you that night, something he hasn't done since 1992.

7. Stop communicating with him for several months after the kiss, then decide to move to San Antonio. Convince yourself you're moving there because with you "can't afford New York anymore," you just need "a change," some "better weather," maybe a "break from winter."

8. Try to ignore the horrors of social media and the documentation in tourist-style photo albums of your love's return to the dating world. (We're not talking porn here, just lots of photos of cute gals in clingy tops beaming in the presence of a tall, dark, and handsome firefighter . . . I mean, I can't blame them, but I *totally blamed them*.)

9. Commit to ignoring him on social media and everywhere else, and begin dating other people.

10. Fall for a bouncer from the Flying Saucer beer joint.

11. Fall for a transplant surgeon from your hospital whose diet consists of doctors' lounge pretzels and Diet Coke.

12. Weaken and occasionally visit your sweetheart, make out with him on his couch, then leave in a huff of indignation and self-loathing while you preach to him about boundaries.

13. Give up on love with anyone and lose yourself to working the night shift.
14. Go out on a date with a Freemason you meet online, though your only real connection is a shared fondness for green tomatillo *salsa verde*. When he hears you are a musician, he invites you to try the pipe organ at the Scottish rite temple downtown "after hours." You decline.
15. Go on a date with the transplant surgeon. He makes you laugh, but you notice a look of distaste flash over his chiseled features as you happily down a tuna melt. He's refused dinner except black coffee. All's not lost, as he's introduced you to the music of John Prine.
16. Block your sweetheart on social media and erase his phone number.
17. Go back to India with the full expectation that you'll rediscover your commitment to global health and only return to the States to put your life in storage and take a job with Doctors Without Borders. But then lie under your mosquito net in the thick, humid heat, no fan, no electricity, and feel overcome by a dull ache in your belly. Fall asleep listening to John Prine's "Speed of the Sound of Loneliness" on repeat. You've been lonely in India before, but this is different. In your twenties and early thirties, flying solo to the other side of the earth invigorated you, but you've changed. If you disconnect now and stay global, will you ever land?
18. Fly back to San Antonio and buy a house.
19. Ignore the no-contact clause with your sweetheart when he texts you about his mom, Rocky, and her prospects for a kidney transplant at your hospital. You've loved his mom since you first met her back in Nebraska in the early 1990s when you both had big hair.

    (Seward, Nebraska, was a town whose women generally followed strict rules of understatement in their appearance. But Rocky wasn't a native Nebraskan. Born and raised on the west side of San Antonio, she had a full head of thick, black hair in cascading, feathered curls; she wore flashy, silver jewelry that jangled from her ears and arms; she used eyeliner and mascara to frame her bright, brown eyes; she donned colorful outfits and jogged through town in bright purple leggings. She turned heads on the square, on the softball field at Plum Creek Park, and in the frozen food section of the Hinky Dinky grocery store. Add to the exoticism my giant crush on her youngest son, Ryan, plus the fact that whenever she saw me she called me "sweetie" and "hon," and Rocky maintained near celebrity status in my childhood worldview.

I didn't know that someone else's kidney had pulsed inside of her since 1978. Ryan was just four years old and his mom twenty-eight when she received her first kidney transplant, a fairly new treatment in the late 1970s. After Ryan graduated from high school, Rocky moved back to San Antonio, to a new husband and a new life. Ryan went with her, to his own first marriage and a career in the San Antonio Fire Department. Soon after she returned to Texas, her first transplant failed and she went back on dialysis. Because of Rocky's high level of antibodies, her body would reject kidneys from 98 percent of potential donors, even Ryan's.)

20. Reply to your sweetheart that you'll inquire about Rocky's case. When you see the Diet Coke pretzel surgeon that evening, ask him about her. He's friendly and recalls every detail of Rocky's case down to the 98 percent rejection stat, and despite your failed tuna melt date more than a year ago, he promises to update you later in the week.

21. Continue to ignore your severed-contact rule when your sweetheart texts you the very next morning and asks "Did you have something to do with this?" because Rocky just got called in to your hospital for a transplant. Against the 98 percent odds, and seemingly overnight, they found a match.

22. Speed back to work and take two steps at a time to the third floor transplant unit to find your sweetheart waiting for you outside room 315. Neither of you will breathe when you hug, so be sure to exhale before going in to see Rocky for the first time in twenty years. She calls you "sweetie" again, and you can't help but laugh when you see the IVs on each of her arms fighting for space among clumps of bracelets.

(Those first few moments with Rocky were tinged with disbelief and wariness. I knew she'd pick up on the chemistry Ryan and I kept trying to avoid; I knew she might not get the transplant in the end—when they call you in, there are no guarantees until they wheel you into surgery—and Rocky had been through this two times in the past ten years and toiled for fourteen years on dialysis. I also hadn't slept since the day before, and I feared that the pretzel surgeon might walk into the room at any moment. Yes, all we shared was an awkward dinner and a year of text/chat/phone romance, but still, he was the closest thing I had to an "ex" in San Antonio, and the convergence of people from my past and my present, all due to the accidental death of an unknowing organ donor in a car wreck on Loop 410 the day before, made me feel like I'd stumbled into some kind of synchronistic minefield.)

23. After Rocky's surgery, become her personal transplant nurse. Visit her every week to review her labs, check her ankles for swelling, and discuss the color and frequency of her urine, an exciting topic for a woman who hasn't peed in fourteen years. Note how her house is filled with wind chimes inside and out—they even hang from the steering column on her truck; how the word *believe* decorates the entire home, from wall plaques over the bathroom sink to magnets on the fridge. In the midst of the grueling reality of dialysis (exhausting and at times painful four-hour treatments three days each week), dietary restrictions, fluid restrictions, a 40 percent mortality rate, and a life expectancy after diagnosis of renal failure of four to six years, Rocky had created a sparkling realm of optimism in her home and daily life. After her transplant, her *believe* focus shifted from kidneys to matchmaking—to Ryan and me.

24. For the first month after Rocky's transplant, keep your sweetheart at a friendly distance until the night he sends you a photo of the two-by-four that had crashed through the windshield of his fire engine that morning and nearly killed him.

25. Sleep with him that night.

26. Sex brought on by a flying-lumber-near-death-experience does not equal a relationship. Though separated for two years now, he's not yet divorced. Break up with him again.

27. Adopt a puppy to fill the void.

28. Paint the sunny yellow walls of your new living room a soft gray called "elephant mist." According to *Real Simple* magazine, "gray is the new white," and the color matches your mood. During those long days of painting quiet, you arrive at the realization that you and your sweetheart may never be together.

29. Give up on love.

30. Keep in touch with Rocky. Introduce her to your new puppy. Listen to her concerns about her son and shrug. When she calls six months after her transplant to tell you she saw blood in the toilet, send her to the doctor. When she's diagnosed with colon cancer, drive to meet your sweetheart at her house. (Side note: Everybody needs to get a colonoscopy after age fifty. Get over your stigmas, do the bowel prep, and go. You'll be sedated, you'll have no idea that a camera is winding through your innards, you won't remember a thing, and it could save your life.)

31. While you stand in your ICU and help your sweetheart feed Rocky ice chips after surgery, listen and listen closely when she says in her scratchy, postanesthesia voice, "All right, you two: if this dumb cancer doesn't bring you together, what will?"

32. Decide you and your sweetheart need a theme song if this relationship is really going to work outside of the confines of Rocky's hospital rooms. Honor the 1980s and go with "Respect" by Erasure (my favorite line: "And if I should falter, would you open your arms out to me?"). When your sweetheart comes to take you on a do-over first date, play the song for him as he drives you home at the end of the night. Dance next to him there in the truck. Sing along to the words, and loudly, but not so loudly that you miss the fact that he's singing along with you. And dancing. This tall Nebraska farm boy is dancing and singing because he loves you, and because his mom doesn't have cancer anymore, and because he knows that when he goes to kiss you at your door in a few minutes, you'll stand on your tiptoes to kiss him back. The two of you have finally reached the beginning.

# 11

## Zombie

If you should ever come to Seward for the Fourth of July, you will find a man named Clark on the stage of the sky-blue band shell downtown, announcing the annual apple pie eating contest. With each round of contestants, he shouts, "What could be more fitting or appropriate than apple pie on the Fourth of July?" Then he instructs them to put their "noses to the sugar" and shouts, "On your mark, get set, EAT!"

Clark, like Mom, is a teacher. Clark actually engages Mom to read the questions at the Seward High School Quiz Bowl each year. Like Mom, Clark is a pillar in the community of Seward, and he loves the word *appropriate*.

What did not feel appropriate to Mom was that Ryan and I slept in the same bedroom on our first visit home as a couple. It was Thanksgiving, Mom and Dad had a full house, and there weren't enough beds for us to *appropriately* bunk separately, despite the fact we were in our late thirties and lived together in San Antonio. This was a Christian home, and we were unmarried. But my parents are pragmatists, so the moral sacrifice was made.

It had been more than ten years since I'd brought a boyfriend home, and it became apparent very quickly that in order for Ryan and me to be together, I had to break up with Mom. What seems like a straightforward, leave-the-nest situation for most did not exist for me. If your primary bond is with your mother, and then your mother leaves you and you redo your primary bond with a second mother, it's a terrifying idea to end that relationship or to transition to a more distant connection because you've shifted your primary bond to your high school band section leader. This is not the work of the frontal lobe. You can't say to Pat, "Mom, I'm in love with Ryan. I want to marry him. This means you have to stop telling me what to do with my time when I'm home. I'm not leaving you, but our relationship needs to change. I'm not going to call you first with my problems. I'm not going to show you my bowel movements before my singing performances. I belong to a new family." After all, I am the grown child who—well into my thirties when Ryan and I reconnected—regularly adhered myself to Mom's bosom at bedtime while she tried to read opinion columns in the newspaper. And she is the mother who mandated her grown daughter's social commitments and arrival times for meals on visits home. She even balked if I spent too much time with Grandma and Grandpa A.

This would not be pretty.

I winced the night I confessed my Mom bedtime ritual to Ryan, but before I could finish, he wrapped his arms around me and said, "I'm not going to give you up for adoption." Until he said that, I hadn't realized how deeply I'd needed to feel kept or how difficult it might be for Mom to learn that I wouldn't be asking her to keep me anymore.

During the holiday weekend, we split time between my parents' house and Ryan's dad's in Lincoln, spending Thanksgiving Day in Seward with the Ohlmann clan. After Saturday and Sunday with Ryan's family, we rushed back to Seward for one last meal before flying out the next morning.

"Want to go for a walk later?" I asked Ryan halfway through dinner.

"What?" Mom said through clenched teeth. "You just got here!" She pounded the table with each word.

"Mom, please," I said. "We were gone a day and a half with Ryan's family."

"Gone all day and now you're going to leave again?"

I was mortified that she would assert her command of my time in front of Ryan.

"And I meant to ask you, Suzanne: who hit you in the face?" she said.

"What?"

"All that redness around your eye. Did someone smack you?"

My eyes widened. Was she accusing Ryan of something?

My brother and his wife sat across from us, chewing in silence, their eyes focused on the pizza. To my right, Dad lifted his empty plate, looked down his bifocals, and reached for a second slice. All seemed oblivious to the volcano erupting at our end of the table.

"No, Mom," I said. "It's called rosacea; it's a stress rash."

"Mm-hmm," she said. "I can't imagine what you'd have to be stressed about."

Ryan had hardened at the suggestion of violence in our relationship, his hands melded to the table, jaw twitching. Though he remained silent, his feelings flashed red across his face and neck. Unlike my family, Ryan wasn't habituated to Mom's brief surges of rage when I suggested I might like to do something outside of her plan, a plan already compromised due to the time we'd spent with Ryan's family. She'd insisted we eat in Seward on the night we arrived, despite the fact that Ryan's dad had driven to Omaha to pick us up at the airport. She'd scoffed at our choice to go to the Nebraska football game at Memorial Stadium on Friday, rather than stay in Seward and watch it on TV with the family. She'd let out a long sigh when I called on Sunday afternoon to tell her we would be stopping to visit a friend's grave on the way home, a classmate of Ryan's lost the month before to breast cancer. According to Mom, the cemetery was "out of the way" and would "postpone suppertime."

Mom and I could clear a room with our frequent and familiar rope-a-dopes, and my takeaway of her message, repeated over miles and years, was a version of "You have not met expectations. You will never meet my expectations." But this time I studied Ryan's hands and their heavy grip on the table. Their presence and strength set a new boundary between Mom and me, and I felt an internal, organizing algorithm change. I observed the observer, and in that moment my out-of-date allegiance to the child-daughter role was finally laid to rest. Though it was a frigid, windy night outside, Ryan and I threw on some long johns and took that walk after dinner.

Five years before that chilly Thanksgiving walk, on my second visit to India, Mili, a tiny girl from the next village over, three years old and bursting with life, knocked on my bedroom door at the hospital.

"Come to my house!" she shouted, her voice squeaky like a kitten's. *Apa ame giba mu gharuku.*

"Where is your mother?" I asked. *Tu bou kwadegola?*

"I came by myself!" She jumped as she spoke, her arms reaching up for a hug. *Mu eka!*

Months before, Mili had been run over by a milk truck, her left foot maimed and only her big toe intact. She'd come to the hospital daily for dressing changes for her wounds and declared to everyone that I was her *apa,* her big sister. I'd often made visits to her village in the afternoons, but this was the first time she'd marched the one-kilometer distance to the hospital alone, and she had done so in the worst heat of the day.

"Does your mother know where you are?" I asked her. *Tu boa janicha?*

"I don't know!" she giggled. *Mu jani nahi!* She'd started up a little Bollywood dance routine in my room. No disfigured left foot could keep Mili down.

As we walked along the dirt road to her village, I dropped back to take a picture, which still hangs on my wall. She's wearing a tattered sundress and a cotton cloth like a hood covering her head. The road spills ahead of her as she strides, her arms swinging freely, her head turned to the left to catch sight of something in the distance. She's fearless.

Unlike Mili, I did not feel fearless when I left my mother. I woke the morning we were to fly back to San Antonio after Thanksgiving in a thick, depressive fog. Though my past bouts of depression had come on over time, this relapse arrived like a thief in the night. I slept in the car on the way to Omaha. I slept on our flight to Dallas, and I woke long enough between flights to call my therapist to schedule an emergency appointment the next day. Ryan had left Texas with his girlfriend and returned with a zombie.

After several therapy sessions, I decided to ask Mom via email for a period of noncommunication. To her credit, she agreed. Christmas approached, and migraines began to come weekly and then daily. I quit my intensive care job, Ryan took over our bills, and my therapist asked to see me twice a week and offered to split her fee.

"Why?" I asked her.

"You're in crisis," she replied.

To ring in the New Year, my birth mother emailed me with the news that my grandma Dolores had died. I'd last seen her during the summer four years earlier. Her apartment had been decorated for the Fourth of July, with swaths of blue and red Saran Wrap draped across her TV console. Not wanting to miss a moment of conversation between Dolores and Leah, when I excused myself to the restroom just down the hall, I kept the door propped open, like a little girl still potty training.

Dolores made a phone call. "Hello, Gladys? Dolores here. Listen, I want you to come over this afternoon. Can you?"

"Mom, what are you doing?" Leah said in a loud whisper.

"Gladys, now just hold on a second. Leah's trying to say something here," Dolores said.

"Suzanne is here!" Leah hissed.

"That is exactly the point, Leah. I want my friends to meet her," Dolores hissed back.

I turned on the faucet to wash my hands.

"I'm not ready, Mom," Leah pleaded.

"Oh, for God's sake, Leah, would you look at her? We should put an ad in the paper for all we went through and the way she turned out! When are you going to be ready?"

I returned to the living room as Dolores got back on the receiver. "Well, Gladys, never you mind. I had my days mixed up. I'll call you tomorrow."

Leah kept her arms crossed, a look on her face like she'd been caught stealing. It struck me then that I was seeing the young, single, pregnant person that Leah was when she had me—that we all are an accumulation of our different ages and each age can appear unannounced, depending on the trigger. The thought of revealing her secret to one of Dolores's friends tossed Leah right back to 1976, and so I threw my arms around her there on the couch, as if I'd been oblivious to the whole Gladys fiasco. She softened, and soon we were back to storytelling and taking pictures. That was the last time I'd seen either of them, despite multiple attempts to connect with Leah. She would acknowledge my attempts but then never find a way to meet. "I've got a lot going on," or "My health just isn't so great right now," she'd write. I guess the two meetings were enough for her.

When I replied to the New Year's email about Dolores's death, I asked Leah if there would be any services I might attend and assured her I would be discreet. Could I send flowers, a gift, or a memorial from an anonymous donor? She never replied.

In the absence of Mom and in the wake of Dolores's death, my depression transformed from a drained, heavy weight to days of crying and paranoid ideation. I'd experienced bits of paranoia during my first round of depression in college. Unlike most twenty-one-year-olds on the cusp of a fulfilling senior year of music making at St. Olaf, I couldn't sleep at night because (1) Princess Diana had died the weekend before school began and I was somehow traumatized by this, due apparently to the close association between midwestern undergrads and the British royal family, and (2) surely an alien ship would land in the soon-to-be-harvested fields surrounding the St. Olaf grounds. Aliens. In Minnesota. Craving information from young Lutherans. It all made perfect sense to my fear-ridden, despairing psyche.

I didn't ever say these things out loud, even when I was in therapy throughout my senior year (thank you, Steve, therapist and bodhisattva, for saving my life) and especially after I went on twenty milligrams of

Paxil, which utterly quashed that phantasmagorical thinking. For the Great Depressive Episode of 2012, I did not go the Princess Di route, nor aliens, but settled into the haunted story of our own sweet bungalow in San Antonio.

When I first moved in, my new next-door neighbors chatted me up over the fence one morning and asked if I'd seen anything "strange." As I shook my head, they launched into stories about the ghosts former owners had seen: prostitutes in feather boas from when the house was a speakeasy in the Roaring Twenties and a teenage boy who had hanged himself in the basement three owners before me.

Wait—a suicide in my basement? Aren't the sellers supposed to disclose this before the inspection? I took my neighbors' stories with a grain of salt, but I also walked through each room that night with a smudge of burning sage.

I painted walls, hung artwork, and gutted rooms down to the original pine shiplap. I built a fence in the backyard and adopted a puppy. I fell in love with Ryan. If the ghosts had a problem with my color palette, or the dog, or the tall, quiet plainsman moving onto the property in hesitant stages, they kept it to themselves. All the pieces of a normal life lived in a single zip code had come together for me. Just like Bapa had hoped, I had found my family. Yet in the months surrounding Dolores's death and my breakup with Mom, I was consumed by despair. Falling in love laid bare all my broken pieces. Worse than threatening to leave, Ryan promised to stay, even as I turned inside out with sadness. The only spirits keeping me awake at night were the shadows of my own dark thoughts. The house was haunted, and so was I.

Then I saw the ghost. I'm no paranormal fanatic, and I have avoided Ouija boards my whole life, but on a gray, chilly morning in late March, two months after Dolores died, I saw the boy who'd hanged himself. The ghost appeared as I shuffled a load of laundry across the basement floor, my eyes still stinging from a morning of sobbing, Ryan on shift at work.

Our basement was a dark, unfinished realm of concrete floors, exposed wood joists, and a lonely toilet in one corner that we used for gastric emergencies we'd rather not share with our romantic partner. We called it the Toilet of Despair. In the opposite corner sat a cobbled-together work space: a pegboard for tools, a bench, and shoddy drywall tearing off in pieces. On humid days, it smelled like rat pee, and a transom window on the west wall gave the cobwebs a spooky, if not unhygienic, sheen. Ryan once found booby magazines from the 1970s tucked behind the pegboard. I avoided the space, except on laundry days, since the washer and dryer butted up to it. That morning I discovered our suicide victim had chosen that area for his final moments. (If I had been him, I would have used the Toilet of Despair, but I have a thing about evacuation.)

I dropped the basket of clothes, mesmerized by the sway of the dead boy's Air Jordans as they passed in and out of a patch of light. He looked grotesque, his head at an unsettling angle from his body, and yet also peaceful, a feeling I hadn't experienced in months. A host of questions sprang to mind: How long did he spend planning his exit? Did it feel weird to use your own belt to extinguish your life? I scanned the basement: no rope. I'd have to go upstairs to get a belt, and that sounded exhausting. Could I use a sheet? Would the ceiling hold my weight? I'd felt in depressions past that I'd understood the desire to die, but I'd never stepped so close that I was using trigonometry to calculate the strength of the joists (and let's be frank, SOHCAHTOA doesn't compute very well in a depressive brain, with all due respect to Mrs. Banzhaf and her memorable trigonometry class).

I caught myself in the quiet analysis of my own death and knew that I'd landed in this house to stand and meet this gruesome yet familiar specter. He forced me to consider a grave choice: hang myself beside him that morning or find my way back to that howling newborn in the middle of Nebraska.

# 12

## Valkyrie

"Better out than in," a surgeon once told me. He'd brought my patient from the OR to intensive care, fresh from an incision and drainage procedure to open an infected pocket deep in her leg. She was a grandmotherly woman who referred to me strictly as *mija*, the Spanish word meaning "my daughter," and who had a head of frizzy, permed hair and large, Ruth Bader Ginsburg glasses that magnified her eyes. The sequence of events in her hospitalization had been strange. She'd presented at the hospital with atrial fibrillation, a heart arrhythmia. Despite all the standard treatments, her heart refused to resume its baseline rhythm. "When's it going to be normal, *mija*?" she'd ask me, her eyes wide as an owl's through her lenses. Finally, an infectious disease specialist ordered a full-body scan and the hidden infection was revealed. The moment the surgeon lanced the pocket, my little grandma patient's heart returned to its normal state. When she woke from the anesthesia, I gave her a thumbs-up.

"Better out than in" became my mantra as I turned away from the ghost in my basement, my suicide planning beautifully interrupted when Pablo and Fu crashed through the doggy door for their morning walk. It's quite possible that the dogs saved my life, but I was the one who had to decipher how to keep living it. There would be no leaping back into the light of day, but a slow and steady trudge through the depression and darkness. I had to learn to walk on my moon.

On the night of my birthday, just weeks after I saw the ghost, I sleep-walked through the house, caught in a dream. I'd been a somnambulant since childhood, especially on vacations and visits to family out of state. Mom once found me at age thirteen on the second floor balcony of our Motel 6, rattling on about how I needed to get my earrings out of the car. In my birthday dream, I wandered the halls of a big hospital complex and into their storage area, on a search for a special box containing the remains of an infant. The hospital staff chased me through the dream, followed by security guards and cops with guns, but I lost them and continued my search. I could see the baby throughout the dream, tiny and swaddled with a little cap on its head. Right before I awakened, I found her in a dark room with tall, stacked shelves. She'd been tucked into an old shoebox, the cap on her head as I'd envisioned. I scooped her up, and as I awakened into real life, I stood at the foot of our bed, rocking back and forth and saying "Shhh, shhh" to the nonexistent baby in my arms.

I didn't grow up paying attention to my dreams, or "navel gazing," as Mom says. My parents can seem more analytical than feeling types, with hungry minds in constant pursuit of knowledge to process and categorize. They come by this honestly. Education is one of the bedrocks of their faith and culture. Martin Luther himself rewrote the Catholic catechism, dividing each of the standard prayers of the church into sections, each clause or commandment followed by this question: What does this mean?

If one is Lutheran and wishes to feel something, one turns to music, another staple of the Ohlmann household. I can still see Mom's excitement the day Pachelbel's Canon arrived in the mail on vinyl. It became a record I often requested (and called "Taco Bell"!) when Jeff and I were little and took turns choosing bedtime music.

I was slow to change my own analytical habits in my biweekly therapy sessions, my therapist constantly cueing me when she'd notice my brow furrow or hear me hyperverbalize my feelings to the point of physical detachment from the body.

"But I don't want to feel," I'd say.

"Not here." She'd point to her forehead. "Feel here," she'd say, her hands at her chest, then at her belly. She was right. My frontal lobe needed to rest.

And so I turned to music, to a section from an opera that made me weep, though I hadn't seen or heard it in more than ten years. I was twenty-four when I attended my first live performance of Wagner's *Die Walküre* at the Metropolitan Opera, and I nearly had to be removed on a stretcher at the end of the final act. There were certainly others in the hall who may have merited medical attention, since we'd been together in that hot room for nearly six hours—*Die Walküre* is at minimum four hours long, with two intermissions between the three acts—but I was a rumpled mess.

The Met was created for spectacle, true to the nature of the art form it presents, and the audience plays its own role. Men dress in tuxedos, women in evening gowns, and you'll never see a show where there isn't someone, or several people, who have decided it would be a good idea to wear a cape. Scarves and jewels abound, and I'd joined the throng, wearing a black velvet dress, my great-grandmother's rhinestone choker, and a red cashmere wrap. I relished my fellow audience members as much as I enjoyed the performance, and I tried not to startle when an audible snore sounded from the warm, plush seats of the hall. But during the curtain calls, I struggled to even stay upright, my scarf a wet muddle of tears.

During the final act of *Die Walküre*, we see Wotan, the god and ruler of Valhalla, enraged at his favorite daughter, Brünnhilde, a Valkyrie (from Norse mythology: a young maiden who rides a winged horse over battlefields to bring the souls of slain warriors to Valhalla), for disobeying him. As she pleads her case, he softens and alters his punishment. Though he had planned to place her in a deep sleep and abandon her to the fate of whomever happened to find her, she begs him to surround her in a ring of fire. He agrees, knowing that only a brave warrior would pass through fire to emancipate Brünnhilde.

The final half-hour of the opera is an extended and heart-wrenching farewell from a parent abandoning his child. From my seat in the fifth row, I could see the spittle launching from James Morris's lips as he intoned Wotan's long goodbye. With each soaring melody, I found myself choking back tears and a sudden desire to add my sobs to Wotan's heralds of grief. I hoped he couldn't see me crying there, so close to the stage, and was grateful his vision was partially occluded by the trademark Wotan eyepatch. (Wotan once gouged out his eye in exchange for a drink from the well of wisdom.)

As the lights came up, the woman next to me offered tissues from her Prada bag and patted my shoulder. She was petite, bespectacled, and for a moment seemed like she might actually be Supreme Court Justice Ruth Bader Ginsburg, a known opera fan. Like me, the woman and her husband had not missed a second of the performance. We'd been together for six hours, long enough to become acquainted, if not friendly.

"Oh, dear, are you going to be okay?" she asked.

I nodded and mustered a thank-you.

"The music really spoke to her," she said to her husband, who studied my plight in earnest.

"So nice to see a young person appreciate Wagner," he said.

They'd driven down from Connecticut for the performance and insisted on giving me a ride home in alternating, patter-style exclamations.

"It's no trouble at all."

"You can't take the train at this hour!"

"It's on the way."

"Come on, dear, you could be our daughter."

As we zoomed up West End Avenue, I'd already morphed back into my sunshine self, with zero interest or awareness as to why I would have been so destroyed by that last scene. But twelve years later, back at our haunted house after therapy, I dialed up YouTube to reexperience "Wotans Abschied und Feuerzauber" ("Wotan's Farewell and Fire Music") and commenced a boo-hoo fest quite reminiscent of the first time I saw the opera at the Met. Catharsis can take decades for the descendant of German Plains farmers. As Kate McKinnon said on *Saturday Night Live* while imitating German chancellor Angela Merkel, "In Germany, we take our emotions and scream them into our stomachs."

No more stomach stuffing for me. *Better out than in.*

Though my biweekly therapy made me feel and music made me weep, I didn't want to end my investigation of my origins stuck in some Wagnerian fantasy. Brünnhilde may be the ultimate abandoned daughter, but she's also the sturdy soprano with blonde braids and a Viking helmet of "it ain't over until the fat lady sings" fame. Like many women of the Great Plains, I've been called sturdy, and though it is perhaps not the most flattering of adjectives, after this period of sad and vulnerable discovery, I wanted to feel like a Viking again. There are no handbooks for repairing one's broken self, I don't care how many *Chicken Soup for the Soul* books exist. If I'd given up the frontal lobe of my educational upbringing and sunk deep into the mythic realm of music and dreams, if I'd opened up Pandora's box and let all the painful moths and locusts free, at some point, according to certain versions of the myth, a tiny dragonfly of hope was supposed to appear.

Nearly a year into my separation from Mom, Dad mailed a ten-page letter written with the theme "How Long, Lord?" Clearly, the noncommunication was taking its toll at home, but I wasn't ready. My heart had become like a neglected room in a big house. Once you decide to clean up the room (in the hope of incorporating it into the home rather than blocking the door and ignoring the stank that occasionally seeps from beneath the floorboards), much like Pandora's box, the heart's room may nearly explode into a painful chaos. Then comes the sorting: trash pile, keep pile, burn out back in a sacred rage pile. I couldn't have Mom close by, reminding me of the time and humming endless hymn snippets.

Hymns aside, as I continued to surface from the depths of depression, I decided to try singing again. I saw that the San Antonio Symphony was performing Mahler's Second Symphony, "Resurrection." I scraped together an audition—it had been five years since I'd nearly puked into my underpants at Mom and Dad's church—and made it into the chorus.

After two months of prep came the final dress rehearsal. As we sat on stage in the rosy light of the Tobin Center for Performing Arts, on the site of the original Municipal Auditorium in downtown San Antonio, just off the famous River Walk, a project built between 1938 and 1941 and made possible by funds from the WPA—Works Progress Administration, thank you, Franklin Delano Roosevelt (I'm adding as many modifiers as possible to this ridiculous run-on sentence because I'm too nervous to admit and thus write the predicate)—I had a vision.

I feel confident in stating that it would not be considered normal conversational material to confess to friends that you've had a vision, especially without the influence of peyote. You can't ask a buddy how the new job is going and then, when they ask you what's new, reply by saying, "Oh, just living the good life and trying to decipher the meaning of the female crucifixion scene I saw floating over the orchestra for a good three minutes last night during rehearsal. Thanks for asking."

Nobody in Seward, Nebraska, talks about visions, not even the Bohemian Catholics just north of us in Butler County. Those folks have kolaches and grottos and statues of the Virgin Mary, but my tribe? No statues. No reflecting pools. No visions. We have doctrine, scripture, and the means of grace. Still, in my opinion, and I have in many ways left the tribe, if a person were to have a vision, the existential, even seismic nature of a Mahler symphony would be an appropriate and fitting setting.

I may be committing some kind of sacrilege here, but the only climax I can compare to the heights of music and sound that Mahler creates at the end of his Second Symphony is a stadium during a football game. The quarterback takes the snap, hands it off to the running back, who breaks a tackle and bursts into the open field. The fans rise to their feet, their applause a steady, swelling crescendo, until a terrific roar erupts as the running back crosses into the end zone, victorious strains bursting from the band when the referees raise their arms: touchdown!

But Mahler's stakes are higher: the final movement of the Second Symphony is a retelling of the end-times. The dead rise to face judgment in a jagged, zombie march, the offstage horns sound, and soon the four trumpets ring from the four corners of the earth. Here at the most important moment in the symphony (and myth of humanity), Mahler turns judgment day on its head. Rather than separating the holy from the damned, God grants the heavenly kingdom to all.

During our final dress rehearsal, after the choir had made its first entrance—on a hushed, almost inaudible intonation of the word *Auferstehen* (resurrection)—the small, powerful, German conductor stopped the orchestra. In a crisp, accented voice, he began to speak to us about the concept of being stigmatized.

His choice of words threw me for a moment. I did not believe in phenomena such as stigmata or ancient relics. (Did you know there were at one time at least eighteen supposed pieces of the *Preputium Christi*, or Holy Foreskin of Christ, traveling around in reliquaries to cathedrals across Europe?) He must have sensed a similar reaction spreading through the chorus, because he paused, threw out his arms as if on the cross, dropped his head, and remained in that position for several weighted seconds. Then he raised his hands so his palms faced us, and he said, "You don't sound stigmatized enough. You haven't suffered enough to merit resurrection. Do you see what I am saying?"

I clutched my black folder to my chest and felt tears coming. I realized the maestro hadn't been talking to me directly, but hadn't I suffered enough? Maybe Dad was right with his How Long, Lord? letter.

*Get it together*, I thought. *You are sitting in a flock of fifty sopranos. There will be no crying.* I took a deep breath, closed my eyes, and there, floating high above the conductor, a crucifixion scene appeared. Three women hung on the crosses, their faces and bodies blurred.

I opened my eyes, but the vision remained, shimmery and fantastical like the migraine auras I dreaded. Though I stayed in my seat on the choir risers, a part of me took flight, ascended into the rafters, and hovered near the women. They came into focus.

Rehearsal resumed, but I stayed with the vision. The French horns heralded the end of time from the balcony. Singers all around me cleared their throats, our first entrance just measures away. But I soared over the orchestra and cried for the crucified women: my two mothers and, in the middle, me.

*Disclaimer: Though I did play the role of Jesus in the sixth grade for our annual Easter chapel (due to the fact that none of the boys in our class wanted the job), I do not have a single messianic impulse in my body. In no way does this vision convey any kind of Branch Davidian future for me or any of the Ohlmanns or Erpeldings.*

Ryan has a way of meeting my psychological explorations with an open mind and a dry wit. During the intense months after my suicidal thoughts, we bought a small, old school chalkboard at an antique store and hung it in the bathroom. My hope was to write a new, meaningful message on it whenever I needed encouragement. One morning I wrote: "Breathe. Be your true self." Later that evening I found he had added his own words: "Put Seat Down."

When I told him about my female crucifixion vision, he said, simply, "Jesus."

Exactly.

Several nights after the rehearsal, he woke to find me kneeling by the bed, reciting an unfamiliar prayer—unfamiliar to him. Though also from Seward, Ryan did not grow up Lutheran. On our first Thanksgiving home, he'd noticed that my family always says the same prayer, known as the Common Table Prayer, before meals. (*Come, Lord Jesus, be our guest, and let Thy gifts to us be blessed.*) Unbeknownst to me, he had begun to commit it to memory. Months later, just after Dolores's death, we were on the cusp of sleep when I asked him if he knew the Lord's Prayer.

"Yes," he whispered.

"Will you say it with me?" I asked and waited for his reply for what seemed like a long time.

"*Come, Lord Jesus,*" he began, and I nearly peed myself. "What? Isn't that the Lord's Table Prayer?"

So when he found me in the wee hours rattling off the Apostle's Creed, he didn't know if I was asleep or awake.

I was asleep.

"Baby," he said.

"*Suffered under Pontius Pilate,*" I prayed.

"Baby," he said, louder.

"*Crucified, died, and was buried.*"

"Wake up."

"*He descended into hell.*"

"Baby!" he said, putting his arms around me.

I gasped awake, unsure of my surroundings.

"It's okay, you were dreaming," he said. He pulled me back into bed. "Tell me about your dream."

We spoke in the dark, awake but in voices quiet with sleep.

"I was home. I was at church, and we kept saying the creed over and over, like on a feedback loop."

"What creed?"

"The Apostle's Creed."

"What does that mean?"

"I have to go home."

"Because of the creed?"

"I have to go where my story began."

"Do you want me to come?"

"No."

"To make up with your mom?"

"That's part of it."

"And then what?"

"I have to forgive Mom, and then I have go to the place where I died, descend to my hell, and find the people who were there."

"Jesus."

Exactly.

# 13

## Fried-Egg Sandwich

Was it a coincidence that country music singer and songwriter Bobby Bare released the song "Dropkick Me, Jesus, through the Goal Posts of Life" (the world's only Christian football waltz) in 1976, the year of my birth? In a sense, my birth mother did dropkick me, proverbially speaking, through the goal posts of life that very same year. Maybe the comparison seems harsh or silly, but I've learned to give myself license when it comes to describing what some refer to as a primal wound. In addition to the song's title, lyricist Paul Craft penned a hilarious line to end the first verse: "If you've got the will, Lord, I've got the toe." Find me a better lyric in all of country or Western music.

How can one of Nebraska's daughters resist both the football and religion in this song? Why not bring a little levity to a story that carries so much weight and sadness? Why not name these final ventures into my origin story the Dropkick Me, Jesus journeys?

I knew my first trip home would be to see Mom and Dad, reestablish contact, and fill in the gaps from a year of little to no communication. I drove up with the dogs and stayed at a La Quinta Inn in Lincoln (no sleepwalking episodes à la Mike Birbiglia, thank you, Jesus) with plans for lunch in Seward the next day.

Mom made fried-egg sandwiches at my request, with white bread, salt and pepper, melted butter, and the yokes not runny and not hard but with that sunny, orangey middle, the way she knew I loved them. Mealtimes at the Ohlmann house nearly always included reading material, but not this lunch. After we prayed, Mom asked me how I had been doing, so I began to share some of my difficulties from the past year (I skipped the part about the ghost). They listened with wide eyes. Their concern encircled me.

I told them of my migraines, depression, and Dolores's death.

I told them my migraines had become so unbearable that I'd had an MRI; that they'd found a brain aneurysm; that I'd had a surgical procedure to look at the arteries in my brain; that the doctor was a Nebraskan; and that when he looked at my brain from the inside, he said he'd found "a series of perfectly healthy, unique twists and turns of the vessels that would look like an aneurysm on a scan." "You're going to be just fine," he'd said. "Go Big Red."

"I didn't want to tell you unless they'd found the aneurysm," I said. They nodded, tears in their eyes.

"I didn't want you to worry. And now we know it from a doctor and fellow Nebraskan: I may be healthy but just not quite right in the head." They chuckled.

I told them they had loved me enough.

I told them how hard it was for me to admit that I wasn't the happy person they'd hoped I was and that what had happened to me before I became their daughter instilled a lifelong fear of separation. Though we'd all been aware of my battles with depression and anxiety, this truth proved the most difficult to admit in their presence. I didn't want them to think they'd failed. I didn't want them to think I'd failed either.

I told them my sadness was not their fault.

Hoping to lighten the mood with a literary reference—these are book people—I shared a quote I'd come to admire from Shakespeare's The Tempest, in which Prospero says, "This thing of darkness, I acknowledge mine."

"Glenn, how does she know all this stuff?" Mom laughed.

Dad puffed out his chest and said, "Well, she is a librarian's daughter."

Later that fall Mom mailed me a letter and surprised me with her own "better out than in" revelation:

Dear Suzanne,

Since our conversations on your visit, especially when you shared some of your struggles with a sense of separation, I have been bothered even more than usual by a memory I need to share with you.

When you were perhaps a year old—I'm not at all sure, but you were already a stinker about bedtime—I put you to bed one night and closed your door as usual. And you began to cry. You cried and you cried and you cried. It was serious, heartfelt crying. And I stood by your door, torn by whether to go in or let you cry it out.

Finally you stopped crying. And ever since I have ached with the memory of that night. Now, I know that I would go in and pick you up and rock you for a long time—and how I wish I could go back and make that choice.

I wonder how awful that must have been for a baby who already had a sense of having been separated from something or somebody.

I am so sorry for that failure of mothering and I hope you can forgive me. I did love that little girl, and I do love the woman she has become.

Mom

When I called to thank her for revealing the story, she confessed she had never shared that memory with anyone. She didn't even tell Dad on that same night after she put me to bed, came downstairs, and joined him on the couch for an episode of *Masterpiece Theater*. I don't know why she kept this secret. Maybe she heard a quality in my cry that resonated with her own experience of abandonment. Maybe she keeps a tight, planned schedule in order to avoid any remnant of those feelings and passed that gift on to me, an unwilling, unable recipient. Maybe she volunteers her time at church and in the community to fill that same sense of abandonment in others. After thirty-five years of tantrums and periodic verbal eruptions, followed by a year of silence, Mom's revelation reached into one of my heart's darkest rooms, opened the door, and said, "I hear you."

# 14

## Thumbs

Two months after the first Dropkick Me, Jesus journey, I headed back to Nebraska for Round Two while Ryan stayed home for work. I brought the dogs again. I needed their humor. I needed to stay grounded. I needed to scoop fresh dog poop into biodegradable bags every morning.

I spent a week driving around central and southeastern Nebraska to try to reunite with the social worker who placed me with my parents (still living, willing to meet), the doctor who delivered me (still living, willing to meet), and the nurse who'd cared for me in the nursery and even filled out my paperwork (still living, willing to meet). All appointments would finally happen on the same day, though in different cities nearly two hours apart. I reached out to Leah in preparation for the trip, hoping to find out where Dolores had been buried. Since her death nearly three years before, I'd found no record of Dolores's grave in any of the local cemeteries. I wanted to pay my final respects. Leah never replied.

On the day of the appointments, I woke at dawn to drive to Lincoln and meet the social worker, the sun rising over the Garland hills as I drove east on Highway 34. Thanks to my dad's fastidious maintaining of family files, I found the social worker's name on the adoption paperwork: Gary Gollner. My dad remembered Gary fondly from their preadoption meetings, describing him as young and handsome at the time, and always believed that Gary played a major role in matching me with our family. Not only did Gary place me in the Ohlmann home, but he was present at my adoption ceremony and had even picked me up from the hospital in Grand Island on the morning of my relinquishment.

After Gary and I settled into cups of institutional coffee in his pale yellow office, I asked him about my relinquishment. He explained it as both a process in which the mother signs away rights to her child and the literal moment in which the social worker takes the baby from the hospital and the baby becomes a ward of the adoption agency. He told me how each relinquishment—he had placed more than three hundred babies during the course of his career—was ridden with such grief that he felt as if he'd witnessed a death. And then, sometimes within a matter of hours, depending on where the baby was born and the location of the adoptive parents, he experienced the adoption, a celebration of renewal, a new beginning. The social worker literally carried the baby across that middle ground, caught between death and resurrection.

Gary paused for a long moment and looked at me with kind, blue eyes. His neatly combed, silver hair sat in a tidy side part. Nerves kept me from meeting his eyes for long, and I focused on the pink ring my Burt's Bees lip balm left on the rim of my Styrofoam cup. His office was chilly, the coffee bitter yet warm enough to bring comfort with each sip. He waited for me to look at him again.

"You know, Suzanne, the only other person who navigated that dark, middle realm—who went from death to life—was the baby. You experienced a death," he said, pointing at me. "That's the reality that always troubled me so deeply. How was the baby affected by the magnitude, the dichotomy of the experience? How could the baby not know what was lost?"

Well, so much for my coffee. I bawled my head off—in deep, uncontained sobs—right there in front of Gary. And when I gathered myself, I thanked him for naming something I'd just begun to comprehend and for being there when it had happened to me. "My dad says you were so kind, so special," I told him. "He was right."

A social worker and counselor his entire career, Gary listened and let me cry.

"You wouldn't be normal if this hadn't affected you, Suzanne. I was there. It's okay to grieve."

He and another social worker, most probably someone named Steve, though Gary couldn't recall for sure, drove to Grand Island three days after I was born. Once at the hospital, they completed the necessary paperwork and carried me out to Gary's brown Chevy Caprice Classic. One man held me while the other drove back to Lincoln. Some babies Gary placed were born in the same city as their adoptive parents, so the time between relinquishment and placement could be as short as hours. From birth to Ohlmannhood, I waited nine days.

Years after our meeting, Dad discovered another set of letters between Gary and my parents. It seems that Gary and I had suffered together, and not just through the grief of relinquishment. Mom and Dad had always told me that my placement with them was delayed because of, as Dad—a man never wont to discuss anything below the waist—put it, "digestive problems."

Mom just said, "Suzanne, you couldn't poop."

It's embarrassing to learn that the very first piece of information your expectant family had about you was that you had dysfunctional bowels. Despite my best efforts to uncover every shred of information surrounding my birth, the fact that Lutheran Family Services had lost my files prevented me from discovering any actual documentation to support my parents' constipation narrative.

As a nurse, I've helped many constipated people, including friends who texted me in great pain and embarrassment and ICU patients whose bowels went on strike after major surgery. I spent the entire twelve hours of one weekend shift making a young liver transplant patient poop, a course of action that involved three different types of enemas, the final concoction made of warm milk and molasses. (I am not making this up, and the results were, as I reported to the physician, "monumental.") Jokes aside, given what I know about constipation in adults and the fact that it rarely occurs in neonates, it's difficult to accept what might have been my plight as a tiny newborn.

Thanks to the newfound letters from Gary, I now had proof, including this excerpt from a letter dated January 3, 1977, when I was about ten months old:

> Thank you for the picture and generous gift. Suzy looks healthy and happy! She has really changed since I last saw her. I still vividly recall the horror of those "purging" trips to the pediatrician prior to her placement with the three of you.

First of all, let's discuss the verb "purging." Was this some kind of medieval pediatrician? Are we talking pre-Reformation medicine here? According to the *American Heritage Stedman's Medical Dictionary*:

**purge** (pûrj)

*v.* **purged, purg·ing, purg·es**
   To cause evacuation of the bowels
*n.*
   1. The act or process of purging
   2. Something that purges, especially a medicinal purgative

When I looked up *purgative*, I found this:

**purgative**
/ˈpɜːɡətɪv/
*n.*
   1. a drug or agent for purging the bowels
*adj.*
   3. causing evacuation of the bowels; cathartic

I did not sense anything "cathartic" in the tone of Gary's writing, and I marvel that more than ten months after the event, he could still "vividly recall the horror."

What was wrong with my tiny baby gut? Most infants don't suffer from constipation until they start eating solid foods around five months of age. Were the Lutherans hypervigilant about my health? Martin Luther relished the activity of his children's bowels and was known to reference his own defecation habits using language that would stun modern congregations into weeks of constipation. Did Gary's Lutherans want to be certain they were delivering a nondefective product? Was it customary in the mid-1970s to purge a seven-pound baby's colon?

After our first meeting, Gary and I kept in touch regularly by email, but he died before I could see him again. How I wish I could have shared his letters with him when we met, as I'm sure they would have triggered his memory. His vocabulary and descriptions in those letters made my body ache for days after I read them. My gut has been a Greek chorus in the narrative of my life, from my constipation when I was just days old to my supposed "barf fountains" (later determined to be the result of lactose intolerance) at my babysitter Esther's house to my continued effort to keep the train station of my belly on a steady arrival and departure schedule. Our guts function through signals from our central nervous system, and I can say now, with proof, what I've always known—that separation from my mother took its toll on my nerves and on those good souls like Gary whose job it was to care for me through the long days between relinquishment and adoption.

When the doctor who delivered me—we'll call him Doc Rogers—agreed to meet, I took the first available appointment. After a month of pining and planning, all the meetings landed on the same day due to everyone's schedule. After I left Gary's office in Lincoln, I drove a hundred miles to the women's health clinic in Grand Island.

I waited to meet Doc Rogers in a patient room, sterile white walls and a cold exam table in front of me, clean paper stretched across its length. When a deep voice boomed outside the door, I shuddered in remembrance, then shrugged it off. I wouldn't actually recognize his voice, even if it was the first sound I heard on Earth, would I? Maybe it wasn't him but someone else in the practice.

But then Doc Rogers knocked and entered the room, a big buck of a man, broad, bearded, and fatherly. He took a stool and sat like a coach, hands on his knees, present but just a touch unsure what I came all this way for after all. I'm the first baby he'd birthed who'd been adopted out yonder and come flying all the way back. He'd delivered thirteen thousand babies, you know. He didn't remember me.

But then he leaped into action, fumbling his giant hands over the phone on the desk to call Janice down in Medical Records to see if they could dig up a shred of our collective past that might just jog his memory. I told him not to get his hopes up with Medical Records Lady. I'd called her the year before, explained my search, and received a good five minutes of chastising for "meddling in the past" and "misunderstanding the basic fact that adoption laws were written to protect the mother." I'd hung up in tears.

Doc Rogers paid little attention to my concern. He was a big man on this medical campus, and there was no reason Janice would shame him out of his request like she had me. Plus, he had his hands full with the phone—he struggled with technology and was missing half a thumb due to a farming accident in his childhood. Twice he disconnected Janice and then misdialed over to the nurses' station on the ward, his chatter checkered with epithets of "dad-blamed!" and "highfalutin!" But he finally got through, Janice located the records, and *poof!* A touch of magic began to dance around that tiny exam room. His once-wary eyes now twinkled, and I leaped up and threw my arms around him. He wasn't expecting a hug.

We broke for lunch, and when I returned, the now smiling Doc handed me my files in a manila envelope and kept my mother's files close to his chest. "Just wanted to compare notes on you and your mom," he said. "You can have yours but not hers."

I pored over the hazy photocopies of handwritten records. I read that I pooped very little and vomited a lot. I read my birth mother's name and address at the time of my birth and the place where she lived while she waited out her pregnancy, a locale I had never considered in nearly twenty years of searching.

Doc Rogers seemed tickled as he watched me read and leafed through my mom's notes. "Just for fun, I'll tell you that your mother was four to five centimeters dilated when she arrived at the hospital at 6:20 a.m. the morning you were born. Three hours later you showed up. 9:27 a.m."

"Really? That fast?" I asked.

"Don't worry," he said. "I didn't squeeze your head too hard."

I rose to leave—he had patients to see—and hugged him again, and this time he hugged me back. Maybe we'd connected after all. I thanked his assistant in the hallway and flew out the door into the gray skies of a Nebraska November, another piece of the puzzle snapped into place.

Mary was her name. Mary, the nurse who'd signed the information page of my birth paperwork. The name was blotted out on our family's copies from Lutheran Family Services but not on the ones the Doc had just given me. Mary had fed me, weighed me, swaddled me. She still worked at the hospital, and she agreed to meet me after an encouraging call from Doc Rogers and my meek, bad-first-date, choppy, stilted chatter when he handed me the phone. These are not conversations for which a person can prepare in daily life or even in a public-speaking organization like Toastmasters. "Hi, so, you were a nurse in the hospital where I was born and left by my mother—on purpose, but still, not an easy thing—and here it is almost forty years later and I just met the doctor—did you know he's missing part of his thumb? Yeah, well, he tried to call you earlier but dialed the nurses' station on the ward, and, well, I'm a nurse too and so we all know how that goes, but anyway, uh, are you around and could we meet, even for a couple minutes?"

She sounded less than enthused at first. Mary had a lot of work to do.

"I'm not expecting you to remember me or anything. I just want to sit with you and hear your voice, but not in a creepy way. I'm just trying to connect with something old—not that you're old—old in me. This is hard to put into words."

She agreed to meet.

Mary was much warmer in person than on the phone. Although the hospital was new, built several years after I was born, and the old one mostly torn down, she gave me a tour of its birth unit and nursery. As we sat in the lobby, a friend of hers came in the door and Mary introduced her to me.

"This is Suzanne, one of the babies I took care of before she was adopted in the seventies. She's come all this way home."

Her friend snapped a photo of us. We sat, our arms around each other, our hands together, the fingers of one of my hands wrapped around hers, an echo of a newborn's palmar grasp reflex. She may not have really remembered me, but I remembered Mary.

As soon as I left the hospital, I looked up Leah's old address and drove through residential Grand Island to find it. After a few nervous moments parked outside the apartment complex, I realized I had no reason to feel anxious. Nobody who lived there now had any idea who Leah was, let alone the secret she kept or the fact that I was the incarnation of that secret. So why not get out and walk around and take some photographs? I strolled the sidewalk surrounding the one-story colonial-style buildings—bleached brick facades with white paint chipping from their shutters, each apartment with its own front-door entrance facing the street—and snapped a picture of Leah's former front door. The buildings formed a U-shape around a kiddie park, and I could picture her there that November, thirty-nine years before, pregnant and bundled up for winter, her toddler son padding around the park, tossing off his left mitten, then his right. A train blows by on the tracks and she reaches down to hoist her son up, counting the cars as they pass. She's nineteen and has already met with a social worker. She won't keep second baby.

My stomach growled as I took in my prenatal home. Tired and hungry, I was glad I didn't have to worry about getting back to any five-thirty suppers in Seward that evening. Mom had changed since our breakup, now more than two years in the past. She'd ask questions on visits home regarding schedule and meals, but only out of curiosity, not demand. Thanks to this change, I'd made my second Dropkick Me, Jesus trip without her shadow cast over the week, free to explore on my own time and in my own car, yet still tuck into bed each night in the guest room down the hall from Mom and Dad.

As I stood there in the park, the sun began to sink in the west, its light filtering through the near-leafless branches of pin oak and maple trees lining the block. A southbound train sounded its whistle, blaring a jazz chord as it passed, tossing my thoughts up into an eastward flight toward Columbus and the trains passing Mom's house, then southward toward San Antonio, to our front porch and the words on our front sidewalk: We always lived close to a train for some strange reason.

After a few loops around the hospital site—the original building was partially torn down and rebuilt into an assisted living facility—I cruised into downtown Grand Island to check out an antique store I'd passed coming into town that morning. I needed to wander through stacks of old stuff to unplug from the overload of information I'd ingested throughout the day.

The place was huge: two old, tin-ceiling downtown stores combined into one antique mall; and stall after stall of Depression, carnival, and milk glass, Hummel figurines, cafeteria tables covered in boxes of antique Nebraska license plates. Ella Fitzgerald sang Rodgers and Hart over the sound system. Pumpkin spice potpourri wafted up by the cash register to cover any of the dank smells from old stuff. And a small group of retired women were hanging Christmas decorations throughout the store, despite the fact that it was still a week before Thanksgiving.

On my final lap around the store, I spotted a plaque on the wall for three dollars. It had a gold, five-by-seven-inch frame with an Art Deco–era painting and a poem inset in fine, Deco font:

## MOTHER

**I know that my Mother prayed that Life might give**
**The sort of treasures to me that will live:**
**I know she prayed that kindly Time might bring**
**Contentment, peace and joy in everything.**
**And what she asked in love has come to be**
**Because her love means all these things to me.**

"Anything else for you today?" a woman chimed at the register. "I just love these old, framed poems."

I smiled, too tired for chitchat but grateful for her Nebraska charm. I knew that I wouldn't always encounter such even, peaceful feelings toward my mothers, but that poem would forever commemorate the day. A sense of calm washed over me. I was eager to tell my mom and dad about it. I wished I could tell Leah too.

"Are you from Grand Island originally or just in town for a visit?" the woman asked as she wrapped the plaque in tissue paper with Scotch tape.

"Born here, but I grew up in Seward and now live in Texas with my husband, another Cornhusker."

"Isn't that neat. When were you born?"

I began to feel love for this woman, with her themed cardigan covered in crocheted autumn leaves, her bobbed silver hair, her bedazzled readers on the tip of her nose. She could have been friends with my mother in Seward and perhaps joined her at Curves for her daily 7:30 a.m. workout. I missed these Nebraska women.

"March twenty-second, 1976, St. Francis Hospital," I said.

"So then you must have seen the cranes, haven't you?"

"The cranes?"

"The sandhill cranes? Every March? My word, you've got to see them if you were born here in March. You won't believe it. They're louder than Memorial Stadium on football Saturday, I tell you, thousands of them out there on the Platte. What day were you born again?"

I'd driven past sandhill cranes throughout my childhood during spring trips to Colorado to celebrate Easter, and I'd seen the tall, gray birds pecking at corn in harvested fields as we blazed by in Grandpa's beige Chevy sedan.

"I was born on March 22."

"My dear," she said as she took off her readers. "That third week in March is when they're at their highest numbers. Half a million come through here from late February through early April. You'll just have to go home to Texas and come right back this spring. Come for your birthday, why don't you?"

# 15

## Flight

The Platte River cuts a swath from west to east across the state of Nebraska, its blue ribbon on the state map resembling a broad smile more than a river. It stretches from North Platte in the west, where the North and South Platte Rivers unite, almost all the way to Omaha on the eastern border, where it joins the Missouri. Settlers once described the Platte as "a mile wide and an inch deep," its array of braided channels flowing nearly five thousand feet across at its fullest, back before homesteaders started using it for irrigation, and before states built reservoirs upstream to harness its waters for supply and power. As the Platte reaches the central plains of Nebraska, it shifts direction from southeasterly to northeasterly, creating a wide, grinning shape on the map, an eighty-mile stretch of river named the Big Bend reach, with the cities of Kearney and Grand Island like bookends along the length of the territory. The Union Pacific Railroad travels along this portion of the Platte, as do the Lincoln Highway and, last in order of construction of the transcontinental transportation corridor, Interstate 80.

Before roads or even railroads, pioneers converged along the Great Platte River Road on their westward routes, seeking gold in California on the Oregon Trail, religious freedom in Utah on the Mormon Trail, or a chance to homestead a patch of prairie on land that wouldn't become Nebraska until 1867. The Sioux referred to the Platte River trails as the Holy Road, in accordance with a treaty signed at Fort Laramie in 1851, an agreement between the plains tribes and the U.S. government to refrain from attacking the influx of wagon trains traveling along the river trails. Before the Holy Road, Pawnee tribes called the Platte River Valley home for centuries, living in permanent earth lodges and in tepees when traveling on their annual spring bison hunt.

But before the Pawnee, the Sioux, and Willa Cather's O! *Pioneers*, the Platte belonged to the migratory birds of North America's Central Flyway. Like the pinch of an hourglass in their annual flight trajectory, the Platte River is a hub for millions of birds each spring as they begin their journeys north, most notably for more than a half-million sandhill cranes. The Big Bend reach provides an ideal resting spot, its shallow waters an overnight roosting site safe from land-bound predators like coyotes. The abundant waste corn on the surrounding farmlands provides up to 90 percent of the cranes' diet as they fatten up for the final leg of their migration.

Whether or not my biological parents ever considered the historical and natural crossroads they inhabited growing up in and around Kearney, whether or not this great intersection of indigenous history, exploration, and ancient bird flight ever entered their minds, the two of them found their way to each other, and on a hot summer night in 1975, probably sometime around the Fourth of July, they celebrated their own convergence and created me.

Mike had already moved on to a new girlfriend when Leah discovered she was pregnant. She packed her apartment in Kearney, tucked her ten-month-old first child into the backseat of her car, and drove east along the curve of the Platte River to Grand Island, to an apartment by the railroad tracks, to a fall and winter of hiding.

Just like Leah during her winter pregnancy, I went into hiding at home in San Antonio after my November Dropkick trip. I could have been liberated by all the information I discovered, could have ridden the waves of all the magic I found in the delivery doctor's office, my birth records now scattered across my desk at home. But I couldn't seem to get past

Leah and her repeated, lovingly worded rejections. Some days I tested the waters of acceptance, assuring myself that I had all I needed. I'd asked all the right questions, and I'd come to as many answers as I'd ever find. Other days I rode waves of resentment and anger. Well-meaning family members asked questions like "How much more research do you think you might need to do with all this?" and "Haven't all your questions been answered?" and "What is it you're looking for? Closure?"

"I don't know, Babs," I'd say in response. I'd given up on closure at about the same time as I'd given up on the Missouri Synod ever allowing women to serve communion or, God forbid, be pastors. (Context: Saudi Arabia is passing laws to allow women to drive and the Missouri Synod is decades away from allowing women to lead a congregation. A local pastor's explanation? "I have my tradition." Ah, yes. As did the slave owners of the South and the human traffickers of the West Indies and the city councils of Salem, Massachusetts, who burned women at the stake for being menopausal or, worse, herbalists.)

Looking for Leah had always felt like a search for lost love. All the clichés of romantic relationships matched the feelings I carried, as if my relinquishment was a breakup, like she dumped me for reasons I couldn't understand and said, "It's not you, it's me." The times we'd spoken on the phone and seen each other had become a nervous blur. Sending her email, even drafting a message I never planned to send, gave me clammy hands and the urge to empty my bladder. But wasn't this normal? Aren't our mothers our first loves?

Despite my blues, Ryan and I made plans to see the cranes on my birthday in March. Of the two sanctuaries that offered guided crane viewing, Rowe Sanctuary and the Crane Trust, I chose the Crane Trust for its proximity to my birthplace and booked two guide "blind" tours in the hidden viewing shelters, or blinds, with spare, bench seats and Plexiglas windows. Just feet from the Platte, we'd hide there to watch the migrating cranes herald the dawn and dusk of my birthday.

With a renewed sense of purpose, and perhaps a touch of inappropriate adrenaline, I named our March crane trip the Birth Do-Over. I would surround myself in clouds of trumpeting sandhill cranes on the morning of my birthday, during the very hours my mother was laboring and delivering me, just miles from the very site where that half-thumbed doctor pulled me into the world. This seemed like a magical way to try to reprogram any traumatic memories or primal wounds. I wanted to discover, in the midst of all those wheeling birds, that I'd been born in the right place, at the right time, and in the middle of something much older and much more profound than a single, human birth.

The closest I can come to describing the call of a sandhill crane is to compare it to a growling jazz trumpet; like Cootie Williams blowing through "Tutti for Cootie," the concerto Duke Ellington composed for him when he was a member of Ellington's band. I could even add the voice of Louis Armstrong to the mix (think early years, like "Dinah"), another warm, growly sound born deep in the throat, yet shimmering with light and power. But even in the company of these jazz legends, the comparison falls short.

Sandhill cranes are tall, lean birds weighing six to twelve pounds, their wingspan six to seven feet across. They flap at a slow, regal pace and make ducks and geese look like bobbling amateurs. Their windpipes are nearly four feet in length, descending down their necks and wrapping around their inner organs—thus their rattling, powerful cry. Their breasts are covered in gray, silvery feathers in scaled patterns. Black, fingerlike feathers cover the tips of their wings and, when folded across their bodies, create a layered cascade at their rear called a bustle. A sandhill crane's forehead, or *crown*, is a scarlet patch of skin that shifts in size depending on the bird's mood and perception of danger, a literal red flag. Cranes are often mistaken for storks, but they differ from storks in several ways: (1) they don't deliver babies to expectant families, (2) they extend their necks during flight, and (3) they have a majestic, trumpeting call that can be heard from a mile away, whereas storks croon a feeble rasp at best.

As we drove into Grand Island on the day before my birthday, we spotted our first cranes just east of town on Highway 34, a small choir poking their sharp, black beaks into the soil, standing together in pairs and clumps, random birds leaping and flapping their wings, a mix of feeding and dancing fit for any social gathering.

Ryan pulled quietly onto the shoulder and dug the binoculars out of the console, each of us then easing our windows open to listen. A mated pair began their "unison call," a ritualistic, synchronized duet between a male and female. The male began the music, his neck pointed to the heavens as he let out his first intonation, his partner immediately responding in a repetitive, piercing echo. I listened in silence and observed how their song spread among the group, other pairs joining in their own duet, a unison call hoedown. We would chase cranes all over central Nebraska for the next forty-eight hours and never grow bored, never tire of the cranes' spectacle and, best, their music.

After checking into our Grand Island motel on the eve of my birthday, we decided to drive out to the Crane Trust, both to gauge the distance and time it took to get there and to familiarize ourselves with the place. The lobby was packed when we arrived, the 6:00 p.m. crane tour about to embark and a busload of Chinese tourists having just arrived unannounced. Surprised by the crowds, we grabbed each other's hand and made a beeline for an empty hallway filled with crane art and photography.

A painting stopped me. Bright, textured pinks, reds, yellows, and oranges covered the canvas, with three crane silhouettes outlined in the foreground. The birds stood in profile, two cranes together on the left side facing a third, smaller crane on the right. Its wings outstretched, the little one seemed to be inviting its parents to dance.

Sandhill cranes are family-oriented birds that mate for life and keep their babies for two to five years before sending them out to find their own life partner. For the first three to four weeks of life, crane babies, called *colts*, sleep tucked into the warmth and safety of their mother's wings folded together on her back. Only death or disease can break the bonds in crane families. And data gathered from cranes that have been banded for tracking and research purposes show that each year the same crane families roost in the same locations along the Platte River, for generation after generation.

I scanned to the right of the work and found a quick bio of the artist, Megan Moffett. She'd named the work *Family Greeting*.

Great. I hadn't gone on the actual crane tour yet and I was already shedding a tear. Ryan put his arms around me and studied the painting for a moment.

"Let's go find your friend Cheryl and buy it," Ryan said.

Cheryl was the coordinator of the visitor center, and I'd spoken to her several times on the phone—first when I'd called to reserve our crane viewing spots, then when I'd called to confirm our spots, and then again when I called to confirm the confirmation. I feared that the things I wanted most in life wouldn't come together or would be a figment of my imagination. I even told my Erpelding family how I worried that the DNA was wrong. I worried that maybe Leah lied about Mike being my father. I worried because I loved them so much and felt such music when we were together, and even though I looked like them and walked like them and am the spitting image of my great-grandmother, Zana Clark, I worried that in the end it would turn out that Mike and Leah weren't really my parents.

I also called Cheryl at the Crane Trust on another occasion—all these calls happening in the span of two months, mind you—to find out how I could confirm that the sandhill cranes actually migrated through Grand Island during the spring of 1976. I blabbed to her about my Birth Do-Over trip and my concern that the cranes might have changed their route for the first time in thousands of years. What if the reason for this whole Birth Do-Over and all the momentum behind it could be disproved because of some crazy scientific anomaly? What if Cheryl discovered that the cranes actually flew through Des Moines the year I was born?

Cheryl looked like the school secretary from *Ferris Bueller's Day Off* and remembered me from our conversations, despite seeming a touch frazzled by the cacophony of Mandarin that filled the high-ceilinged lobby. We followed her toward a back office as she prattled on about cranes this and cranes that, and then she suddenly stopped, flanked by a pair of taxidermy prairie chickens in eternal mating dance formation, the bulbous, orange sacs on their throats fully inflated.

"You know," she said, "I thought of you the other day because I was reading this article about mothers and babies. It said that after birth and for the rest of her life, the mother carries cells from the fetus in her body and vice versa for the baby. They are a part of each other forever. Can you believe it? Isn't it amazing how God made us?"

Cheryl posed between the chickens, blinking her eyes at us in rhythmic thrill.

Ryan and I stood agog, like she'd smacked us on the head with a baseball bat. I wanted to honor Cheryl's proclamation, as well as our prairie chicken witnesses, and dance in stutter steps around dear Cheryl just like the chickens do each spring, my ear feathers raised, the orange sacs at my throat blown up like balloons. Oh, to isolate the cells that cry out within me, to view them under a microscope, identify their origin, give them some fancy, scientific name like *Stigmatis maternis*, and finally prove the presence of this wound within me that I can't seem to heal!

"I'll mark that painting as sold for you two," Cheryl said and fluttered back to her post in the lobby.

Before sunrise we parked on a quiet dirt road, one car in a caravan of birders with their headlights dimmed. Once out of our cars, we gathered around Bob, our guide from the Crane Trust. A retired farmer dressed in navy coveralls, with white wispy hair and clear blue eyes, he whispered directions in clear, sparse words, a touch of wonder in his manner. In the pitch black of predawn, a gust from the south forced our hands into our pockets. I heard nothing but cranes.

We walked in silence through tall, bluestem grass, the world all stars and wind as we tiptoed on the crunchy trail, the beam from Bob's muted flashlight our only guide. Just steps from the Platte River, Bob stopped and uttered a quiet exclamation:

"Good Lord. There's the bison."

We looked up to find a small heard of bison grazing ten yards from the trail, their forms like ancient standing stones, hushed but for the puffs of steam they exhaled audibly into the cold, morning air. We continued toward the river, the cranes surrounding us in sound clouds of melodic chatter. When I asked Bob about their noise, he answered in a hoarse whisper, "Oh, it's never quiet. They sing through the night."

Safely in the blind, a rough, wooden structure about ten feet deep and twenty feet wide, we chose our lookout spot and, for a better view, gently opened the clear, Plexiglas window facing the river.

Ten feet from our window, the Platte coursed at a good clip, its water an undulating stream of silver against the black of the banks and the sky. Everything appeared in variations of gray, and as the sky lightened, the sandbars I had taken to be islands amidst the Platte's braided channels began to move. They changed from fixed ribbons of land to stirring, audible organisms, thousands of cranes roosted together in one stretch of river.

When the first hint of a wide, gleaming sun appeared at the horizon's edge, the sky transformed from a pale blue-gray to glowing bands of rose, magenta, and purple. The cranes, black silhouettes against this radiant canvas, took flight from their island roosts, first in groups of two or three, then in quartets and quintets, families synchronized and soaring into the day. As the sun rose, the sky gifted its warm colors to the river, the whole view from the blind a celebration of saffron, orange, and red. I couldn't decide what overwhelmed my senses the most: the vivid colors or the increasing volume and timbre of the cranes' cries as more families took to the air, thousands still awaiting flight.

A pair and their colt passed over us, and a chorus of calls in pinging echoes descended into the blind. Soon another family passed over, this group caught in a moment of silence, the only sound the air rushing through their wings between slow, rhythmic beats.

I tuned my ear beyond the crane's morning concert to hear the songs of red-winged blackbirds perched on surrounding russet grass and western meadowlarks on the budding branches of nearby cottonwood trees. Soon a flock of snow geese glided past, a migratory V-shape in constant, shifting motion, their honking a sonic complement to the cranes still rising from their roost. In the closest channel to the blind, a floating lump of wood became a beaver swimming past and I elbowed Ryan to draw attention to its perfect, chunky shape. As I gazed to the south across the Platte, line after line of cranes crowded the horizon en route to breakfast.

Half the initial group now gone, the remaining thousands communicated in a collective hurry, eager to leap into the day. Over the course of what must have been several minutes, they gathered themselves in flapping numbers, their chattering cries now a chorus as loud as the finale of Mahler's Second Symphony. They circled the roost like a giant, living funnel cloud, wings and air and sky in layered, sonic momentum. And then they were gone, their calls still close as they ascended a distant wind.

After the dawn tour, Ryan and I drove west on Highway 30 to our next stop on the Birth Do-Over tour: the annual Crane Watcher's Breakfast at the Gibbon American Legion. Gibbon, a town of around eighteen hundred people, is known to most as the home of Rowe Sanctuary, another crane haven, and known to me as the birthplace and childhood home of my birth mother. We were giddy from our sunrise with the cranes, and we filled the car with our own failed attempts at crane calls.

"Gaa-RRRRRROOOO-AH!" I yelped.

"Yikes." Ryan reached over to cover my mouth.

"Let's hear yours, pal."

He rolled down his window and pulled to the shoulder, cranes surrounding us on either side of the road, dancing through the fields.

"What are you doing?"

"Research." He leaned his head out to listen.

The cranes were atwitter, their coffee-klatch chatter a continuation of the first sounds we'd heard before sunrise, pairs and groups passing over us from a thousand feet up (and higher!).

"Don't you wonder what the hell they're talking about out there?" I asked, feeling the urge to script some dialogue for their antics. Each signal from one bird elicits a reaction in kind from her partner, though exaggerated and amplified, an exercise in shared enthusiasm.

I repeated my question about crane conversations to Ryan at the American Legion, where our only company was a table of veterans in hunting gear and one other pair of lonely birders, a sure sign we had the date wrong for the annual breakfast. Our waitress confirmed this when she took our order. She was a friendly, quirky gal who had been in an animated monologue with herself when we first arrived, as she tangled with the coffee maker behind the bar.

"Do you ever feel like we have our radios tuned to the right frequency?" I asked Ryan.

"Frequency for what?"

"For everything. For life!"

I had ample coffee on board and my knees jitterbugged under the table. I'd had some great birthdays, but this one topped the list, and it wasn't even nine thirty. My feelings were confirmed when I saw our waitress buzzing around and talking to herself, complete with facial expressions and raspberry lip trills each time she rang up a check at the cash register. I loved the table of veterans behind us, especially the guy with his back to me. He wore full camouflage hunting garb and had a metal neck brace with traction attached at the shoulders, apparently the only thing keeping his head upright so he could take those sips of Folger's Classic Blend. I loved the birders to our right, with their collapsible, UV protection sun hats, chin straps engaged under the chin. I loved Nebraska and Highway 30 and the Platte River.

"This trip sure seems that way, right?" Ryan said. He, too, was watching our waitress and her entertaining flight. You'd think the place was packed, the way she was jazzing around.

"Maybe I'll ask her about my biological grandfather. This is a tiny town; she's sure to know if he's still alive."

"Ask who?" Ryan said.

"Our waitress."

He cringed.

"Okay, I won't." I shrugged.

"Just tell me his name and I'll look him up. If he has an address, maybe we can do a drive-by. Let's not stir up any old scandals."

"I am not a scandal."

"Fine, but you're leaving here in four minutes. Your grandpa has to stay. Spell his name, would you?"

"Brrrrpppt." I stuck my tongue out, imitating our waitress.

After a glare from Ryan, I spelled out the name, he keyed it into his phone, and the quirkster dropped off our glorious pancakes.

As I dove into my birthday short stack there in Gibbon, my mind wandered to a crane's-eye view of our location, noting the Platte River to the south, the east-west trail of the old Lincoln Highway just to the north of us, and parallel to that, the Union Pacific Railroad, nearly one hundred trains passing through town each day.

These are the same roads, the same rivers, the same tracks that pass through Columbus, Nebraska, my mother's birthplace and hometown just ninety miles east. The tracks carry the same trains that passed by Grandma's house. The same whistles that blew in my mother's ears as a child, and later in mine, sounded in my birth mother's ears here in Gibbon, all day, every day.

"You get that address, baby?" I asked.

Ryan settled the check and we left to do some quick private investigating before we turned west toward Kearney. I dialed up the address on my phone and guided Ryan north into town, over the railroad tracks, and onto a little side street that dead-ended under the viaduct, a short block of tiny houses from a John Mellencamp song.

"There it is. That's the right house number," I hissed, leaning forward to try to make out the name on the mailbox. A Welcome Spring! flag hung by the front door.

Ryan slowed as I balanced my camera out the window and snapped a photo of the name on the mailbox.

"Should I do a U-turn at the dead end and then another quick drive-by?" Ryan asked.

"Great idea, just one more pass," I nodded, my heart pounding in my chest.

Ryan eased forward and crept past the house while I leaned out the window, memorizing every detail. I saw a woman on the back porch.

"Stop the car," I said.

She sat, elbows on her knees, head bowed, a thin plume of smoke wafting up from a cigarette.

"Let me just do a U-turn here."

"Stop the car," I said. "Stop the car right now!" I pounded the dash.

Ryan shifted into reverse and began to make the kind of three-point turnabout that would do Mr. Arneson, our high school driver's ed instructor, proud.

"It's Leah. It's my mom. Will you please stop the effing car!"

I jammed my thumb trying to unlock the door. I was ready to do a dive-roll onto the pavement.

"But don't you want to talk about this? Think about what you should do?"

I swung open the door. "There is nothing to think about!"

By the time Ryan came to a full stop, I was halfway through the yard.

She didn't notice me at first, eyes fixed on some blank spot at her feet. Nearly seven years had passed since I'd last seen her. She wore a royal blue Texas Rangers T-shirt and black yoga pants, her short, cropped hair nearly white.

"Can I help you?" she asked, and I realized I was unrecognizable in my stocking cap and sunglasses. I tore them from my head.

"It's me," I said. "It's Suzanne." I stopped the moment I uttered my name, my fear caught up with my adrenaline. "I'm so sorry, I didn't know I was going to see you today. I didn't plan this. It's just that we came here to see the cranes and, you know, it's my birth—"

A wail from deep within her interrupted my speech. She braced herself on the porch railing for a moment and then limped down the steps toward my place in the grass. She could hardly walk, her hip stuck, her gait jagged and arrhythmic, but she came to me and pulled me into her arms, and for the first time ever, we cried together.

I tried to explain why I was there, but she hushed me and held me closer.

"It's been so hard. I know it has," she said as she limped back to the porch, her arm linked with mine. Our steps matched as we walked around the house to sit on a curved concrete bench in the front yard.

Trains passed, and we talked.

Cranes flew over us, calling and singing, and we talked.

Ryan took covert photos from the truck, and we talked.

She still wasn't getting enough sleep. She was grieving. She'd lost her mother, her mother-in-law, and her husband in the past three years. She needed to sell her house. She needed a hip replacement. She was in too much pain to work, and her fingers, each bent at the first digit, showed the wear of years on a factory job. Her kids were grown, grandkids thriving, and she'd moved in for now with her daughter's family in Lincoln. Everyone knew about me, even her husband before he died. No more secrets, but not much curiosity to meet me from anybody. She'd come to Gibbon to care for her elderly father for the weekend.

I wasn't sure her dad knew about me, so I didn't bother to ask about meeting him. Leah could have suggested it if she'd wished.

I asked her about my birth father again, how they met, why she didn't tell him about me, and if she ever saw him using heroin. I didn't hesitate to ask; I was so relieved to be with her and to have the opportunity to listen to her story.

"He was a real turd, you know," she said, a trace of laughter in her voice. She looked like someone who didn't laugh enough. "We were joined at the hip for a good part of that summer you were conceived, but by the time I knew I was pregnant, he'd run off with another gal. As far as the drugs go, I never saw him actually use it, but that stuff was at all the parties, right there on the kitchen table with the salt and pepper."

Again I was struck by the clear, alto tone of her speaking voice and the gentle rhythm of her diction. She apologized for never following through on my requests to meet, and all I wanted to tell her, then and for the rest of my life, was that she was okay; that we were okay.

After a while, I beckoned to Ryan to come join us, thrilled to have my two nearly lost loves meet for the first time.

"You sure found a nice tall one to marry!" she said, which made Ryan blush. "And you asked about Mom and where she was buried? Well, I'll tell you. She's right here in the house."

"In this house?" I balked.

"I know it seems kind of weird, but yes. We've just not been able to find a place to bury her the last three years, so we've got her ashes in a box we found at Dollar General, cutest little box with leopard print—right up Mom's alley, even the mortician agreed—and we're keeping her here until we can make a decision."

Ryan stood still, biting his lip. If I had looked at him for more than a second, I would have peed my pants.

"But aren't your parents divorced?" I asked. "What would Dolores say if she knew she was in your dad's house?"

"She'd kill us! But it's not up to her anymore, and she'll never know the difference. We'll figure it out one of these days."

Ryan stepped back to take some pictures and my mom and I leaned in, our arms around each other's shoulders. We stayed that way for an extra moment, a train racing past, no point in trying to talk over its roar. As it eased into the distance, a line of cranes flew over us, three pairs, their wing beats matched. We squinted up toward the birds, blocking the sun with our hands, a comfortable silence growing between us as we listened to their haunting calls.

"You know, I've always loved the cranes," Leah said. "For as long as I can remember, I'd take a pair of binoculars with me in the car and, if I had a chance, drive out to watch them in the fields."

"Really? Well, this is my first time seeing the cranes up close," I said.

"This is your first time? You came up from San Antonio just for the cranes?"

"Yeah, to celebrate my birthday with the cranes in Grand Island, like a do-over from the first time, you know?"

"Wait a minute, Suzanne. Is today your birthday?"

I put my head on her shoulder. "Yes, today is my birthday."

"I thought it might be today. Happy Birthday, sweetheart. Happy Birthday."

And it was.

# 16

## *Baseball*

And we all lived happily ever after. (Except for Mike, of course, but I had one more chance to find what he'd left behind, one last Dropkick road trip to make.)

Ryan and I kept being married and, on most days, loving it. We stumbled into some grief when we discovered we couldn't conceive a child, but those clouds have mostly cleared. Our brood of cats and dogs keeps us busy, and some day we may even consider adoption.

Mom and I are back to enjoying each other from several states apart, as well as occasional, mostly friendly bickering when we're together. Our disagreements flare over benign topics such as whose recipe we're using for the corn salad on the Fourth of July.

"Mom, it's Aunt Gayle's."

"I thought it was Rolene's, from Bible study."

"It says 'From the kitchen of Gayle McGriff' on the recipe card."

"Well, Rolene makes the same salad."

"Fine. How many Fritos do I add?"

(This "salad" truly calls for a bag of Chili Cheese Fritos.)

"Well, Suzanne, it calls for a whole bag, but that seems exorbitant."

"Right, Mom, let's be conservative with our Frito distribution."

"Don't get smart with me, daughter!"

Though I don't have a daughter of my own, I've been the nanny and babysitter for many children over the years, some of them as strong-willed and tantrum-prone as I was. I think of my mom in the midst of these outbursts, the most recent by a close friend's toddler grandson whom I watched at a resort hotel and conference center while the rest of his family attended a wedding. When he realized his grandma had left the scene, he erupted like Vesuvius and threw down in a hallway filled with Christian military families setting up for a weekend convention, right underneath the "Welcome in Christ" registration table. Shoes flew, tears burst from his eyes, and I had no choice but to look like some violent mother tangling with her demon-child as I grasped for an arm, then a leg, and then finally pulled him up from the paisley carpet and tossed him over my shoulder, all while his primal screams drowned out the Michael W. Smith album those nice people had piped over the hotel speakers. An angry child can make any parent look bad.

Though Mom and I have been through a series of emotional battles, I have never considered her a bad mother or a bad person. Mom and Dad are both, to their core, good people and great parents. They show up for others in need, they volunteer their time, they donate their money, they meticulously recycle. These are Meals on Wheels people. CASA (Court-Appointed Special Advocate) people. Go-to-Walmart-to-purchase-overnight-sanitary-protection-for-elderly-friends-in-nursing-homes people. And they use coupons when buying said pads to save their friends money. In the midst of their lives marked with service and kindness, they've never taken themselves too seriously. If they're playing a game of cards, you can hear Mom's cackle from the next room. I used to send them postcards with thanks incorporated into every message, and Dad finally pulled me aside and said, "You need to stop thanking us. We did only what parents are supposed to do." I may walk the earth with a good dose of Erpelding rumbling in my genes, but the Ohlmann way of life marks my course at every turn—from music to nursing to writing to laughing at myself.

With the exception of my cousin Chelsey, the Erpeldings and I see each other every couple of years, usually when I visit their place in Kearney, and Uncle Greg and I text each other during Nebraska football games. Chelsey and I have become the yin to each other's yang, and we communicate often, sometimes daily. I dreamed that my search for my birth mother would bring me a woman who knew me without explanation; who sensed my needs and understood my motivations without question; who embraced me with a quiet, earthy, goddess love, and even laughed at my jokes. This is the stuff of fairy tales. This is the mother figure born of an orphan fantasy. And in my case, I also wanted her to be witty and beautiful, and to make her own strawberry rhubarb jam from berries she cultivated in her garden and rhubarb she hacked at the stem from along the west side of her house. The person I describe is not my birth mother, but she is Chelsey.

I'm not so sure Leah and I lived happily ever after. We both expressed a desire to develop a more normative communication pattern, but neither of us knew just how to accomplish that. A year after our sandhill crane birthday reunion, I spent a month in Nebraska for research and writing, and I emailed her upon my arrival. I knew she'd moved to Lincoln, and I was there, too, cat sitting, writing, and waiting for her reply. With each day that she didn't reply, my gut threatened violent protest, until I finally launched into an irritable bowel jihad. I bought so many ointments and tinctures and potions to administer to my inflamed southern regions that I began shopping at different drug stores so the clerks wouldn't look upon me with pity. I confessed my plight to my mother as we washed dishes on a weekend visit to Seward. She was distressed to learn that I hadn't heard back from Leah, and she'd been familiar with my belly's storytelling from the beginning.

"Mom, I feel like my butt is going to fall off," I told her.

"I find Preparation H to be quite helpful in these situations, Suzanne."

Mom and I were more alike than I had imagined.

Leah emailed me back the day before I left, nearly four weeks after I'd first written. That night we spoke for several hours on the phone, mostly about her other children. That's how our conversations lean. They are her world, and rightly so. Though I don't blame them, I find it odd that not one of my five remaining siblings has ever expressed interest in meeting me or even asked Leah about me. It's a lonely minefield. For the sake of my soul, and my sacral-gluteal skin, I don't reach out so much anymore, except for an annual birthday text. I recommend Gold Bond with Lidocaine as well as Pat's Preparation H salve; and anyone with my problem should carry a tube of vitamin A&D cream and some baby powder when they travel. I'll stop there.

I packed more than butt cream and baby powder for my final Drop-kick journey. I'd crossed every person and place off my list except the impossible person, Mike, and his place, Arizona. To experience Mike's Arizona, I had to go through Karen, his ex-wife, the other woman in the love triangle of the summer of 1975—the one Leah left in order to save a shred of her dignity and hide her pregnancy.

Uncle Greg introduced me to Karen via email, and we wrote for over a year before I found the courage to make the trip. What I needed was an excuse, so I told people—and when I say "people," I mean at maximum two coworkers and one friend, even though we all know that people who would pass judgment on a person who spends her time chasing down her life's mystery exist only inside the Caverns of Self-Loathing inside her head—that rather than drive north to see the cranes again for my birthday, Ryan and I were headed west to catch some spring training baseball.

A baseball game gives a person time to ponder. While the conscious mind considers pitch count, balls versus strikes, or the infield shift on the designated hitter who bats left-handed and pulls toward right field, the subconscious brain, safely nestled in the hum of the stands, the smell of peanuts and popcorn, the tunes from the organ, the sudden CRACK! when ball meets barrel, settles deep into processing mode. I needed baseball when I drove to Phoenix to research Mike's addict life and untimely death, so I planned our trip around spring training and the Kansas City Royals.

Our Nebraska hometown is a three-and-a-half-hour drive from Kansas City, so we became Royals fans by geographical default (though my grandpa Ohlmann lived in Iowa and taught me to love the Cubs in the days of Sandberg, Grace, Dawson, and Dunston). I was nine when Mom and I played catch in the yard every night before the 1985 World Series broadcasts, and when I'd get a double or triple during a softball game—I had a clean swing until I started facing those tornado-armed fast-pitch players in ninth grade—my coach called me George Brett. When I lived in New York, I walked from my Washington Heights apartment to Yankee Stadium across the Macombs Dam Bridge. I worked in music in New York and sang with a harpist by the last name of Duffy, a friend and fellow baseball fan. She'd rave about her young cousin Danny and how well he seemed to be developing as a high school baseball player, with pro scouts marking his progress at practice and tournaments.

Ten years later, on a clear, March evening, two years after our crane adventure, Ryan and I paid twenty-five bucks a ticket to sit four rows behind the Royals' dugout at Surprise Stadium, the Arizona desert sun setting as the first pitch was tossed. The Royals' ace, Danny Duffy, along with Hosmer, Herrera, and fan favorite Salvador "Salvy" Perez, were out for the World Baseball Classic that weekend, but oh well. I'd see my friend's cousin another time, and my seat gave me plenty of glimpses of Royals Manager Ned Yost's ruddy cheeks.

My dad, Mike, lived his later years in Chandler, a suburb on the opposite corner of Phoenix from Surprise. Ryan and I had spent the day of the game with his ex-wife, Karen. That morning we met and confessed over breakfast tacos how nervous we'd each been for the day. She was especially worried about revealing "too much" and how I'd react to some of Mike's "truths." I assured her that I already knew many of the unsavory details of my father's life and that, as an intensive care nurse, I'd worked with patients with the very same disease process, addictions, even hair styles (think Bob Seger). This made her laugh.

"I don't want you to think your father was a bad person," she said. "He just had a big addiction problem, one I couldn't solve."

"He also had a mullet," I said.

"The whole time I knew him," she laughed.

Karen and I were going to get along just fine.

Though I'd traveled solo on all of my family research trips, with the exception of the sandhill crane birthday surprise, Ryan and I decided that he should come to Arizona. By nature he'd rather sit in silence than chitchat, but his quiet presence comforts me, and I could tell he'd put Karen at ease, too, as we ate through our messy tacos and wiped hot sauce from our chins.

After breakfast we sipped coffee and talked about Mike and Karen's romance. She said the first time she saw him, summer of 1975, he was wearing flag pants. A friend noticed her watching him strut his stuff and told her, "That Mike is good looking, but stay away. He drinks too much."

But Karen couldn't resist. He'd fallen for her the same summer he was dating my biological mother, unbeknownst to Karen. My uncle still describes Karen and Mike's relationship as "soul mates," and it became clear to my mother that Mike had moved on, so she skedaddled, and we know the rest of that story. Karen and Mike dated. They married. They had a baby girl prematurely, and she died. They moved to Arizona to start over. Mike's drinking consumed him.

"I brought you pictures of your dad," Karen said, digging through her purse. "And your sister."

This was more than I'd considered—I'd never thought of Mike's lost daughter as *my* sister. The first photo showed Karen and Mike at some kind of reception, happy and snuggly together at a table. The second was Mike kneeling next to a baby in a swing, with an oxygen cannula tucked into her tiny nose. My shoulders sank as I studied the two of them, both gone, and too soon.

I have a friend I used to sing with named Conal, a talented pianist and bass player who is notorious for one-liners with an off-the-wall, if not off-color, twist. When we'd perform together, after the audience applauded, he'd say, "Suzette—you hear that? Not a dry seat in the house." He's also famous for saying, "I don't care what anyone says, Suzanne, I think you're great," and for ending phone calls with "Copulator!" or "Hope all is well up your end!" I thought of Conal during our day with

Karen, because I'm not sure any of us ever stopped crying long enough to dry our eyes, or our seats, for that matter.

After breakfast Karen guided us to Mike's old neighborhood, his trailer park, and past the hospital he visited so frequently as the cirrhosis began to unfold. Though she had left him nearly ten years before his death, after their breakup she continued to take him to the doctor, bring clothes when he was discharged from the hospital, and accompany him to his DUI court dates. "He didn't really have anyone else," she said. As she shared a cluster of sad stories over the course of the day, which she told with warmth and concern, an intimacy was born between us. I caught myself sitting too close to her, and I noticed her looking too long at me when the conversation paused.

"You're the very best of him, you know," she said as we ate lunch.

I chewed my bite of sandwich and felt Ryan's hand on my leg. My aunt, Mike's sister, had said something similar the one time we met several years before my Phoenix trip.

"You make the room feel the way he did—full of life, so ready to laugh. Mike always made the people he was talking to feel good, no matter who they were. You do that too."

I thanked her. I'm from the Great Plains, a subculture uncomfortable with accepting compliments. It's an even more challenging task when you're being compared to a person you never knew and you share his genes, even look like him. It made me shiver.

"Sorry if you catch me staring at you. You just feel like him. I can't really believe you're here," she said.

I couldn't either.

Karen's version of my father was that of a lost love and a lost cause, not unlike the Royals' batting and pitching that night at the game. It struck me as I sat in the blue haze of the stadium lights how nice it would have been to chase down Mike before he'd died so we might have gotten to know each other over the long, steady tempo of a ballgame. If what Karen said was true and Mike "felt" like me, why couldn't I have had just one chance to share a bag of roasted peanuts with him, slap him a high five after a home run, maybe laugh together as we watched Ned Yost kick a little dirt at the home plate umpire over a pitch that was clearly outside the strike zone?

I don't even know if Mike liked baseball. It's hard to remember to ask questions about hobbies when you're the newly surfaced daughter trying to piece together even an outline of the man's life. Sports, favorite ice cream flavors, cars, movies—they come later, if ever. His obituary said he'd enjoyed working with his hands. My uncle had given me a tiny piece of doll furniture, a dresser, that Mike had made from a kit. There was also the "mail order problem," which meant he'd left behind shelves chock-full of miniature gas pumps and John Deere and Texaco "collectibles." They'd even found packages unopened at his trailer after he died. He must have watched a lot of QVC.

Thanks to Karen, I learned a few more details:

First of all, the flag pants.

Together they had an owl collection that she kept after he died.

He loved 1970s rock 'n' roll (think Bob Seger).

His car at the time of my conception was a pea green Chevy Vega wagon, and due to the fifth of whiskey he'd left in the dash, bad wiring he'd neglected to fix, and a hot Nebraska summer sun, it burned to the ground in front of Karen's parents' house one afternoon while she was at work. Her sister called her.

"You'd better get home," she said.

"How come?" Karen asked.

"Mike's car is on fire."

"Where?"

"In front of the house."

He'd gotten a series of DUIs, most of them on their baby daughter's birthday. At one point he'd been sentenced to jail time, but because of his asthma (another new fact), he couldn't breathe the stiff air in his cell. He was sent home with an ankle bracelet.

Karen believed that Mike knew he was going to die. During his final months, he'd call a buddy to go out at night, take cash from the bank, and go to the bar across the way from his trailer park.

"The girls all knew him. He'd give them money—extra for the ones who were single moms—and say, 'Just dance with me; please, dance with me,'" Karen said. "Can you imagine the loneliness? How hard it must have been to not have anyone to give you a hug?"

After we left Karen, we drove back to the area where she'd thought Mike's bar had been. We found no bar, but the owner of the barbecue shop down the block pointed us toward Sonny's, a strip club, and the reality clicked into place. Maybe Karen had known that Mike frequented Sonny's when she'd told me of his paying the girls to dance, and I just didn't comprehend the story. Even the BBQ guy looked at me funny as I stood there mouth breathing. Ryan had figured it out, but he went to the Public School Downtown. Those kids understand life's sinful proclivities the way we Lutherans recite the Apostle's Creed. I needed Ned Yost to kick a little dirt in my face and wake me up.

Much like my brain in Chandler, the Royals were getting shellacked by the Oakland Athletics that night at Surprise Stadium. I hardly knew the Athletics but for *Moneyball*, Jose Canseco, and the near tragedy of starting pitcher Brandon McCarthy when he got pinged off the mound by a line drive years ago. He wandered off to some other team, and I continue to wonder: How in God's name did he get back on the mound?

The woman next to me in the stands—Joyce? Norma? I couldn't hold on to much in the way of first names after the day with Karen—was a retired nursing home manager from southern Illinois. She kept stats on the back pages of her program the way Grandpa and I used to do during WGN broadcasts of Cubs games. When a broken bat came flying toward us and landed, somehow safely, in the lap of a gentleman with a cane and a Korean War veteran cap, my seatmate and I rattled off tales of other baseball injuries we'd seen over the years, mine of Brandon McCarthy.

(Ryan was at the game, too, but I refer you to the earlier discussion regarding sitting in silence versus chitchat. He is, after all, the descendant of German farmers who spent long hours each day alone, walking fields of beans and wheat with a hoe, a corn knife, and the sound of their own breath. We are a good match.)

"How can a person return to a place that caused him so much pain?" I asked her. We shook our heads, eyes fixed on the game, the A's filling the bases.

Then again, maybe baseball players are like myths. Maybe they're out there playing the game as a means to show us the best (and worst—see Rougned Odor vs. Jose Bautista or, God rest his young soul, the many and various bench-clearing fights of Yordano Ventura) of ourselves. I don't know. I'm no ace pitcher bravely returning to the mound after a line drive, a brain bleed, emergency neurosurgery, and a long year of recovery. But I did go to a place that unearthed an old, primal sadness, and I stumbled into the bewildering realm of grief for a person lost too soon and, strangely, a person I had missed. I still grieve my father, and I grieve having missed him. All that's left is myth.

After lunch, Ryan drove Karen and me to Mike's former trailer, number 275 at the Sunshine Valley Mobile Home Park on South Arizona Avenue. The window of his bedroom, the same room where he'd died alone ten years before, faced the lane where we inched past. I had found the courage to get there but not to knock on the door. I didn't have the words to try to explain to the new tenants just why I might be knocking and what I hoped to see. Bright white petunias burst from under the trailer's foundation, almost audible in their act of blooming from such an unlikely place.

I couldn't say this out loud that afternoon, but what I really wanted to do was dig a shallow space beneath Mike's old bedroom, sidle past the corrugated metal skirting, and lie underneath his home, his floor, his deathbed, maybe forever. Shallow grave or no, I didn't want our time with Karen to end. In her presence, I felt Mike shift from my biological mythology to a person who actually lived and died on Earth. She'd loved him, married him, left him. She'd born and lost his child. She'd shown up to meet me, an unknown entity until I popped up in her email inbox the year before. She said things like "I want you to think of me as another mother, because I would have loved having you as my stepdaughter." But Karen suffered chronic hip pain from a car accident she'd had with Mike decades before, and she had begun to reach her threshold of physical pain.

At least we had baseball tickets. I'd planned the game as a bookend to the day, a distraction, a place to sit and watch grown men in stirrups spend hours of their life flashing hand signals of vital, competitive import. Unlike major league stadiums, spring training ball parks are free of the overstimulating information binge of the jumbotron. They hark back to a baseball of times past; to a life free of text alerts, push notifications, and status updates about what kind of salad your best friend ate for lunch at Panera.

Each year, commissioner Rob Manfred endeavors to shorten the length of the game, for fear of losing fans whose attention spans can't muster focus for a dry nine innings when each team only scores once. No more pitching out for a walk. No more batters dancing through the obsessive-compulsive routine of removing and replacing their gloves between pitches. No more Salvy visiting Duffy on the mound multiple times during a long at bat.

I needed the andante tempo of baseball that night. Life is as complicated now as it was when baseball began in the mid-nineteenth century—some would argue more so, both for us as individuals and for society. Spring training baseball gave me the space to sort through the thorny truths I'd unearthed that day. If I'd been left to consider the new information with my conscious mind, I'd still be under trailer number 275 in Chandler.

But baseball gave me hours of peace, a broken bat, and the base-stealing mojo of Lorenzo Cain. The pace, the cool air drifting over the fresh, spring grass, the quiet calculations of the managers, and the elation of the fans when the Royals sniffed at a rally late in the seventh inning took me to a place outside myself while the stories of Mike sunk into my bones. The game is as complex as anyone there to watch it, but if you're a spectator, baseball offers you the privilege to forget, at least for nine good innings.

Saying goodbye to Karen that afternoon made my stomach churn, but the nurse in me could see the pain in her hip betrayed in her occasional wince and increasingly strained gait. I didn't want to let her and all she knew about me—and the Mike in me—go, but I put on my game face and tried not to crush her in my arms when it came time for hugs. After a long squeeze, she placed her hands on my shoulders and said, "Your father was a good man."

I nodded and took her hands. She told me she loved me, stood on her tiptoes, and kissed me on the lips. She kissed me as the stepmother she would have been, and I'm pretty sure she kissed Mike too.

# Acknowledgments

To my editor, Courtney Ochsner, for her belief in my voice and her knowledge of what you can and cannot put in a deep freeze. To my agent, Gail Hochman, for her kindness, candor, sage advice, and humor. To Sandy Crump, my copyeditor, whose vision guided this book to its final incarnation. To Linda Harris, who first told me I was a writer. To Bev Donofrio, the midwife of this book as I drafted through my MFA at Wilkes. To Ted Kooser, who wrote me back when I wrote him a letter instead of doing my writing assignment, and then quickly became my Uncle Ted. To Naomi Shihab Nye, whose dervish enthusiasm and front porch visits get me out of bed to write. To my kindergarten teacher, Maxine Fiala, who taught me to read. To my high school English teacher, Maxine Moore, who taught me to love reading. To my college professor Alice Hanson, who shouted me out of the passive voice and called me to describe life in an active voice. To Leah, my birth mom, and Mike Erpelding, my ghost dad, who made me. To Glenn and Pat Ohlmann, who made me a daughter, a reader, and a writer and who still laugh when I misuse words like *genre*. To Ryan, who believed I could do it. And to Chelsey Erpelding, forever my person.

Opa Nobody
by Sonya Huber

Pain Woman Takes Your Keys, and
Other Essays from a Nervous System
by Sonya Huber

Hannah and the Mountain: Notes
toward a Wilderness Fatherhood
by Jonathan Johnson

Local Wonders: Seasons in
the Bohemian Alps
by Ted Kooser

A Certain Loneliness: A Memoir
by Sandra Gail Lambert

Bigger than Life: A Murder, a Memoir
by Dinah Lenney

What Becomes You
by Aaron Raz Link and Hilda Raz

Queen of the Fall: A Memoir
of Girls and Goddesses
by Sonja Livingston

The Virgin of Prince Street:
Expeditions into Devotion
by Sonja Livingston

Anything Will Be Easy after This:
A Western Identity Crisis
by Bethany Maile

Such a Life
by Lee Martin

Turning Bones
by Lee Martin

In Rooms of Memory: Essays
by Hilary Masters

Island in the City: A Memoir
by Micah McCrary

Between Panic and Desire
by Dinty W. Moore

To Hell with It: Of Sin and Sex, Chicken
Wings, and Dante's Entirely Ridiculous,
Needlessly Guilt-Inducing "Inferno"
by Dinty W. Moore

Let Me Count the Ways: A Memoir
by Tomás Q. Morín

Shadow Migration: Mapping a Life
by Suzanne Ohlmann

Meander Belt: Family, Loss,
and Coming of Age in the
Working-Class South
by M. Randal O'Wain

Sleep in Me
by Jon Pineda

The Solace of Stones: Finding
a Way through Wilderness
by Julie Riddle

Works Cited: An Alphabetical Odyssey
of Mayhem and Misbehavior
by Brandon R. Schrand

To order or obtain more information on these or other University of Nebraska Press titles, visit nebraskapress.unl.edu.

CPSIA information can be obtained
at www.ICGtesting.com
Printed in the USA
LVHW011120190222
711485LV00009B/577